What People Are Saying

"Rob Peck's guidebook is chock-full of wise suggestions and down-to-earth advice on how to navigate the shoals of daily life. Reading it is definitely worth exploring, and is sure to give you a few good shortcuts!" —Rich Parker, MD, Associate Professor, Harvard Medical School

"Rob Peck has been a go-to-guy in the things-that-fly category of my life for a decade. I have seen him bring laughter and love to some truly sour situations. I'm so glad he's finally brought his wit, powerful storytelling skills, and profound insights to a format I can carry in my toolkit for a better (and funnier!) life. Reader, buy this book. It won't teach you to juggle knives, but it may slice through some of the self-damaging stunts you're already pulling off." —Boysen Hodgson, Communications and Marketing Director, ManKind Project USA

"*It's a Juggle Out There* is a delightful, insightful, and practical guide for dealing with life's daily demands, dilemmas, and distractions. It's filled with fresh perspectives, humor, and hope. You are going to love this book!" —Alesia Latson, Leadership Development Expert, Author of *More Time for You*

"Rob Peck is one of the most joyful and effervescent persons I know. He has written this book for people like me who need to learn the secrets that have made his life a joyful journey. When the details and complexities of everyday life seem overwhelming, it is important to get a good dose of Rob Peck because what he tells us to do, and how he tells us to be, is the prescription that we need for healthy survival. This book gets two thumbs up from me!" —Tony Campolo, PhD, Professor, Eastern College, Author, Baptist Minister and Spiritual Advisor to President Bill Clinton

"Peck has created a masterful work of motivation, and made it so ful fun that you're laughing all the way to your new and improved life. I you're a fan of clever wordplay, you have hit the literary jackpot with book!" —David Glickman, CSP

"What do you get when you put together common sense, wisdom, humor, and activities that are immediately actionable? This book! It's a must-read for the overloaded and overwhelmed—and isn't that just about all employed people, parents, and anyone else between the ages of 18 to 88?" —Marjorie Brody, CSP, PCC, CPAE National Speakers Association Hall of Fame, Founder and Fearless Leader of BRODY Professional Development

"Rob's wit and wisdom will bring a smile to your face and new insights to your thinking. In short, punchy chapters, he provides the anecdotes and actions that lead to a better quality of life." —Mark Sanborn, Author of NY Times Bestseller, *The Fred Factor* and *You Don't Need a Title to Be a Leader*

"Rob Peck is one of most creative speakers and writers on the planet. This book will spellbind you with its message, the same way Rob's keynote captivated attendees at the National Head Start Annual Awards Dinner. I've co-led Stress Buster Boost Camps with Rob, and I know firsthand how much his insights on Kind Management lead to a better balanced life. Buy this book, and give yourself and your loved ones the gift of a brighter future." —Steve Saffron, President, Saffron Perspective, Inc.

"No juggling is required to hone the craft of right living. Rob's book serves up an artistic, healthy, and humorous outlook on the human journey of life. He inspires us to find hope and happiness, create caring and curiosity, experience serenity and sleep, and offers pragmatic tips to cultivate laughter and love of self." —Bonnie Bolz, Waldorf Master Teacher

"This book is loaded with practical tools for coping with overload. Rob Peck is both a brilliant student and a brilliant teacher, with a droll wit that keeps you turning pages. You won't have to worry about falling asleep reading Peck, but you will be challenged to make the changes he recommends with a juggler's masterful prose." —Dr. Sidney B. Simon, Professor Emeritus, University of Massachusetts, Author of *Values Clarification, Getting Unstuck, Forgiveness* (and 15 others)

"Rob Peck's work is fresh and rings true. Implement the ideas in this book and you will be rewarded with less stress, less guilt, and dare I say it, a better night's sleep! Enjoy and live deeply in the moment, it's all we have." —Chris Reagan, President, Get Ahead Pro Speakers Bureau

"This zany journey through one special juggler's irreverent but practical look at what makes life work is well worth taking. Chapters are light, fun, informative, and fresh windows into insights worth exploring. *It's a Juggle Out There* comes at you with humor and insight that will keep the book off the shelf and in your hands. If you need a fresh take on mastering resilience, finding peace, and living with a zest for life, even when you drop a few balls, this book is a must-read." —Dr. Terry Paulson, Author of *The Optimism Advantage*, Past President, Cavett Award Winner, Hall of Fame Member of the National Speakers Association

"I love the way Rob Peck plays with words and offers original insights in ways so clever they are easily recalled when an 'ego-mergency' arises! A fun read, this book will help you to remember to be more mindful and more 'kindful.' No doubt some of his new words will be entered into *Webster's*." —Lynn Durham, RN, Well-Being Coach, Speaker, and Author of *From Frazzled To Fantastic!*

"With delightful wit and a unique way of seeing the world, Rob's guidebook leads us from worry to wisdom, and teaches us how to lighten up instead of tighten up! *It's a Juggle Out There* will replenish your spirit with an uplifting feeling that no matter how many balls you have in the air at once, you have what it takes to keep them in rhythm." —Brian Biro, America's Breakthrough Coach, Author of Amazon.com Top 100 Bestseller, *Beyond Success!*

"This is a clever, yet profoundly meaningful book, filled with actionable strategies. Rob's thought-provoking ideas provide fresh perspective on how to recognize and grab onto what is truly important, and what to let go of." —David Avrin, Author of *It's Not Who You Know, It's Who Knows You!*

"*It's a Juggle Out There*, couldn't have come at a better time for me. I am recently retired, and have felt overwhelmed and disillusioned. This book has been a godsend! With Rob's wonderful sense of humor, his words have challenged me to examine my priorities and make changes in my outlook on what's important in life. This book is a fun read, yet very thought-provoking and life changing." —Wes Page, Media Arts Professor, Modesto Junior College

"Whether Rob is reflecting on the joys and challenges of life as a single parent, adventures overseas, encounters with legendary personalities, or an afternoon at the swimming pool, his insight and wit move through these essays with a rhythm akin to his impressive juggling routines. Rob's musings will entertain and surprise you. At the same time they probe you to look in the mirror, turn just a bit and see what could be if you gave this kind of attention to your own everyday moments. Enjoy the ride!" —Amy Swisher, Director of Public and Community Relations at Baystate Franklin Medical Center

"Peck has isolated gigantic problems most of us over-busy people need to confront. The concept of keeping multiple objects moving in the air is a perfect metaphor for what most of us deal with day-in and day-out. Rob Peck, a master juggler on the stage, will teach you to be a master juggler in life." —Shep Hyken, President, National Speakers Association, Business Expert and New York Times Bestselling Author of *The Amazement Revolution*

"Rob Peck's book is a metaphorical travel guide on how to live a full and balanced life. It seamlessly weaves together practical advice from a rich combination of modern thought leaders, ancient philosophers, and the eye winking spirit of a court jester." —Jeff Boudro, AVP Talent Management at The Hanover Insurance Group

"Rob Peck delivers valuable insights and strategies to handling the real challenges of life. His engaging and straight forward writing style makes this a very worthwhile read. I love his questions of introspection and implementation. Read this book and you will go beyond juggling to mastery." —Lisa Ford, Author of *Exceptional Customer Service*, CSP,CPAE, National Speakers Association Hall of Fame

"Some people are compelling speakers, some are inspiring authors, and a few can juggle with amazing dexterity. But how many can simultaneously motivate audiences to flourish at work and play, while writing a book about the thunder of a waterfall, the peace of a pond, and the Zen of fishing? I only know one, Rob Peck. You can see for yourself on YouTube, attend his life-changing seminars, and read this book—the one you're holding—and start applying his wisdom today." —Christopher Queen, PhD, Dean of Students, Continuing Education, Harvard University

"Rob Peck's new book, *It's a Juggle Out There*, is a rollicking feast of self-help tips and insights. Taking the savvy smarts that have made him a top performing juggler for the past forty years, Rob turns his keen eye to the balance of life. Rob balances words, ideas, and insights as deftly as he balances his juggling balls. You'll find a wealth of thoughtful inspiration, as well as solid techniques for bringing perspective and intention into our daily lives. With wit and flair, Rob provides a valuable guidebook to the self-care we're all seeking." —Diane Ripstein, CCO, Ripstein Consulting

"Rob's book, *It's a Juggle Out There*, made a huge impact on me! As an educator/speaker, I liked his stories, real examples, and practical tips. As a coach, I found his introspection questions a great way to apply his ideas to my own world and help me with my Kind Management. Be kind to yourself, inhale this book, exhale, and apply the ideas, and you too will see an impact in your world." —Patrick Donadio, Business Communication Coach and Speaker, Author of *Communicating with IMPACT*

"Would you like a bit of levity coupled with improvement in your organization or life? An especially adept and humorously creative writer, Rob's offerings will bring you to a relaxed and reflective state of equanimity. His writings are guaranteed to improve the mood and morale of you and your people, while providing a strong message of teamwork and interpersonal sustainability. Utilize Rob's offerings! Enjoy an instant vacation with good laughs while receiving very meaningful tips on improvement." —John Broucek, President and CEO, New England Natural Bakers, Inc.

"Rob Peck has written a powerful handbook for dealing with life's inevitable bumps, challenges, and uncertainties. It's practical, inspiring, and a must-read for anyone seeking a balanced life." —Susan Friedmann, CSP, International Bestselling Author of *Riches in Niches: How to Make it BIG in a Small Market*

"In his new book, Rob Peck proves he is as skilled and artful shaping words as he is manipulating objects. This book delivers sage and practical wisdom in a way that is a delight to digest. It is extremely well organized, compelling, and useful to anyone wanting to rise above the noise of life and discover a kinder way to live." —Dan Thurmon, CSP, CPAE, President, Motivation Works, Inc. Author of *Off Balance On Purpose*, Hall of Fame Speaker

"Rob's framework of inspiration, introspection, and implementation is very user-friendly and very creative. In this modern age of too-much-technology, he breaks it down in an engaging voice that offers some concrete tools to help unravel an overstimulating world." —David Roth, Former Artist in Residence at New York's Omega Institute (and Two-Time National Anthem Singer for the NBA's Michael Jordan-Era Bulls, whose CD's include *Practice Makes Progress*, *Irreconcilable Similarities*, and *Rising in Love*)

"Rob Peck juggles words and wisdom like flames, amazing his audience with the ability to manage seeming chaos with ease and grace. In particular, Rob breathes new life into aphorisms, placing them into the context of his life philosophy in ways that bring revitalized relevance and meaning. In addition to entertaining with his hearty humor, he also provides hands-on skills through helpful prompts on intention, introspection, and implementation at the end of each chapter. Rob's words work magic, transforming negatively charged triggers into positive electricity to power a more purposeful life." —Bill Baue, Co-Founder, Sustainability Context Group, Co-Founder/Chief Engagement Architect at Convetit, Advisory Board Member at Center for Sustainable Organizations

"At last, this funny wordsmith puts out to the world a book full of wisdom garnered from years of good living. *It's a Juggle Out There* takes the reader on a playful and heartfelt journey into the numerous challenges we each juggle, and encourages us to become the selves we long to be. The book is beautifully organized; each chapter kicks off with a touch of wit and wisdom, guides us into the topic with a simple and powerful metaphor, carries us along with inspiring and humorous prose, invites us to hold up a mirror to our own lives, and then gently offers us an opportunity to identify small steps to make our life better." —John Porcino, Storyteller, Musician, Author in *Spinning Tales, Weaving Hope*

"In *It's a Juggle Out There*, Rob reminds us that it's easy to get overwhelmed, but happiness is our choice. Practicing Kind Management, learning to live with intent, and noticing the spaces between the balls we all juggle every day will lead to a more fulfilling existence. It's sound advice, written in the author's true voice (seriously, I felt like he was reading to me). Give yourself a gift and read this book, but not too fast. Take time to enjoy the journey." —Alan Berg, North America's Leading Speaker and Expert on the Business of Weddings and Events

"Rob has combined his wit and wisdom into an insightful volume that reminds us that angels fly because they take themselves so lightly. Between laughs you will be encouraged to take deep breaths and bring balance into your struggle to juggle it all." —Eric Phelps, Vice President of Development, National Collegiate Inventors and Innovators Alliance

"In our hyper-paced world, *It's a Juggle Out There* helps you keep all of your balls in the air. Rob shows that success can be found by staying centered, having a good sense of humor, and looking at obstacles as gifts. And this book is a gift to anyone who is worried about their balls dropping." —Stephen Shapiro, Author of *Best Practices Are Stupid*

"Rob Peck has hit all the balls out of the park! *It's a Juggle Out There* is an insightful and fun-filled guide to the timely topic of how we can stay ahead of today's many stresses. Rob provides practical and helpful suggestions that are interlaced with humor, humanity, and always contain an eye wink of humility." —Gary Cannon, Headmaster, Cape Cod Waldorf School

IT'S A JUGGLE OUT THERE

A Guide to a Better Balanced & More Fulfilling Life

Rob Peck

Zestworks • Amherst, Massachusetts

It's a Juggle Out There
A Guide to a Better Balanced & More Fulfilling Life

© 2014 Rob Peck
Zestworks Publishing
978-0-692-24585-9

Contact:
Rob Peck
Zestworks Speaking, Training, & Consulting
36 Woodlot Road
Amherst, MA 01002

(413) 834-3459
www.zestworks.com
robpeck@zestworks.com

No part of this publication may be reproduced, stored in a retrieval system, or transmitted, in any form or by any means, electronic, mechanical, photocopying, recording, or otherwise, without the written prior permission of the author.

Printed in the United States of America

Dedication

To my beloved daughter: Jazmine Iris Rose Peck. There isn't a person on the planet who is more important to me nor anyone anywhere who more consistently brings out my better angels. I'm so fortunate to be your father (a role my own dad, Arthur Peck, taught me well when I was a boy).

To my devoted partner: Jeannette Marie Tokarz. It's a good thing you're a doctor. Your wise counsel assisted this book from the moment it was conceived, helped me through each trimester of its gestation, and single handedly saved the subtitle from a miscarriage.

To my closest friends: Charles Silver, Gary Cannon, and John Porcino. I'm so blessed to have two best friends who I've known since boyhood, who were the best men at my wedding, and since the birth of my daughter, a third who has been, and continues to be, the brother I always wanted.

To my dearly departed mother, Judith Ellen Steinberg Peck: Your body is buried but your spirit comes to me on quiet mornings, and softly whispers encouragement. I miss you Mom. But I know in some mysterious way you're still believing in me, and I can hear your voice when your daughter Wendy sings, and see your creativity in your daughter Amy's creations.

Table of Contents

Foreword

By Daniel Burrus

What lessons can you learn about life balance from a juggler? In a way, we are all jugglers, juggling what often seems like the maximum number of balls. Think of the work ball as a rubber ball, if you drop it, it will most likely bounce back. Some of the other balls such as your spouse, kids, family, and friends are made of various thicknesses of glass and if you drop them, they might shatter. Putting even more stress on our daily juggling act, we all know someone will toss us another ball, increasing the possibility of dropping them all. In this world of hyper change, having a balanced life seems increasingly impossible, but as you will find out from reading Rob Peck's book, it's not.

Can you remember the first time you touched brail? It was most likely in an elevator when you were a kid. And the moment you took your finger away from the patterned bumps, I know the first thought that raced into your head: "How can anyone read that?" But with a little more thought, you realized blind people already possessed everything they needed, which was to develop their sense of touch beyond what you and I have done.

You already possess everything you need to live a balanced, well-rounded life, but like a blind person learning to read brail, you need to learn how to develop the skills you need to live the best life possible. With wit and wisdom, Rob will teach you how to handle constant change and actively shape a better life balance.

The accelerating rate of change is as certain as the sun rising in the east tomorrow morning. From education to health care, agriculture to manufacturing, it will burst through every industry and every institution like a technological tsunami. *It's a Juggle Out There* wryly reminds us, "Technology is often simultaneously the solution and the source of our stress. Computers help us work faster, but keep us working longer."

It wasn't that long ago that people left their laptops behind when they went out for dinner or to visit friends. But today we have our computers with us 24/7 in the form of smart phones and tablets. We know we shouldn't check status updates, but we do. It's almost like the priority is not what we're doing or who we're currently with. The priority is whatever's happening through the device. Of course, deep down, we know that's not true. But is our behavior reflecting it?

A friend of mine knows his children are getting older, and his window for taking a driving vacation with them is going to close fairly quickly. So he recently got them all together for a cross country trip. After they returned I asked him how it went. He said, "It was a good trip. We didn't talk much though." I asked how that was possible since they were all in the car together for days on end. He explained, "We all had our various music devices with us, primarily our smart phones and tablets, so we were all listening to our own personalized music list the whole time."

They had an opportunity to have a family conversation, to reconnect on a personal level, and even to play some driving games, but they didn't. I hope they get a second chance, and take to heart Rob's recommendation to "make leisure less about being online, and more about real-time social bonding through shared stories, and true two-way conversations."

Technology can bring us together or pull us apart; it depends on how we use it. The key is in knowing when it's appropriate to plug in and when it's time to unplug. Otherwise, our life is just a blur that is constantly driven by our machines. And as Rob wisely reminds us, "24/7 instant connectivity sounds great, but there's no way spending day after day in a flat out sprint leads to a life that's well-rounded."

We have recently entered a time of technology-driven transformation. This is a good example of what I call a Hard Trend, a trend that *will* happen. And when I look at the three digital accelerators; the exponential advances in processing power, digital storage, and bandwidth, it is easy to see that transformation will accelerate every year. The Soft Trend, the trend that *might* happen, is what will you do about it? How will you react to it? This is something that you and I can influence. We all have an amazing capacity for inner transformation. The Soft Trend is, will you develop it and use it.

In a world filled with uncertainty, it is important to ask yourself; what are you certain about? One thing I'm absolutely certain about is that the future is all about relationships, and good relationships are built on trust.

Rob's stories teach us that in order to form great relationships, we have to begin by trusting ourself first, and that requires taking time for introspection. He points out, "The people who do well professionally — and personally — wisely recognize that downtime is found money; a chance to relax, a moment to pause and reflect, providing vital replenishment."

In my latest *New York Times* bestselling book, *Flash Foresight*, I encourage readers to carve out a one-hour block of time every week where you unplug from the present, and plug into your future. After all, you will spend the rest of your life in the future, you should take a little time to think about it, to shape it, and to make it a better place than it would have been had you not thought about it.

It's a Juggle Out There provides guidance and tools to be actively creating a better tomorrow, instead of a more chaotic tomorrow. Rob invites us to recognize that the more our technology transforms, the more human our world needs to become. He knows there are no shortcuts to lasting relationships. As he puts it, "For all the hype about smart devices that let us do more in less time, the bottom line is shortcuts can short circuit intimacy.

Chapters like "Centering & Savoring" reinforce the value of unplugging and giving attention to the right things at the right times. In Rob's words, "Smartphones are modern marvels, but there's nothing antiquated about putting down the iPhone and making eye contact."

It's a Juggle Out There concludes with a short sampler of Rob's creative writing about nature and the nature of relationships. If you enjoy being outdoors as much as I do, you'll find a lot to savor in this collection of original songs, stories, and poems.

After reading Rob's moving story about his daughter's kindness, I recalled a day when I was out in the yard and a young boy from my neighborhood came walking toward me, crying. "What's wrong, Tommy?" I asked.

He told me that his dog had died. Then he looked up at me through his tears and said, "Mr. Burrus, do you think there are dogs in Heaven?"

I thought about trying to give him some religious or theological answer, but quickly realized it would be over his head. I opted to focus more on his heart. I looked into his eyes and asked, "Tommy, would heaven be heaven without dogs?" He thought for a moment, nodded slowly, and gave me a warm smile. "Thanks, Mr. Burrus."

Sometimes the best answer is a question.

The book you are about to read is a great guide for shaping a better, more balanced life. Enjoy!

~ **Daniel Burrus** is the author of six books
including the *New York Times* bestseller,
*Flash Foresight: How To See The Invisible and
Do The Impossible.*

Preface

This book is the realization of a goal that's eluded me my entire adult life. The fact it's finally come to fruition is a big reason to rejoice. Frankly, it's also a big relief. I can see the headline now: "Record Case of Artistic Arrested Development Finally Reaches Favorable Conclusion."

But I digress.

All my life I've wanted to write a book. When I was a boy, I loved to read adventure stories, and the time it's taken for me to go from reader to writer has been a doozey. It's taken more than half a century to get to this point. To be exact, I'm sixty years old, but I refuse to tell anybody my weight! Oh alright, if you insist: I'm five feet, six-and-a-half inches, and if your brain just said, "Tall," that's the only time that word's ever been associated with my height!

But I regress.

Which is precisely why it's taken me this long to make progress on my boyhood dream to be a published author. Between self-deprecatory jokes and self-sabotaging standards, I've managed to be my own biggest nemesis (giving the biblical credo, "Love thy enemy as thyself," a whole new twist!).

But I persist.

Somehow by dint of sheer determination, and a lot of loving encouragement, this long deferred dream has come true. In the process, the principal lesson I've learned (and forgotten, and relearned repeatedly) is that aspiring for perfection is a prescription for endless striving and postponed accomplishment. In short, searching for just the right sentence structure got me nowhere, slow.

It's like I was living in self-imposed purgatory. A vicious cycle where perfectionism breeds an infernal procrastination (the writer's equivalent of eternal damnation!).

What finally freed me to embrace the truism, "Done is better than perfect," was to lower my expectations and reframe my purpose. Instead of aiming to shoot out of the gate with a rising star publication, I made my peace; whatever I put out would be a simple two-wheel bike, not a NASA rocket ship. After a few spills, and near head-on collisions with my own ego, I realized I couldn't ride a two-wheeler without training wheels.

Writing this book humbled me (a rare example of the understatement I so greatly admire in other authors and so seldom succeed in emulating!). Thankfully, by releasing my penchant to polish, I've pedaled far enough to publish. It hasn't been a smooth ride, but it got me to the point where this prose is ready to travel. The training wheels are off. (Look, Mom... no hands!)

Acknowledgments

This is my first book. The process from conception to completion was both a labor of love and like giving birth to a Bison! Mercifully, I was surrounded from the start by a gifted support team.

My heartfelt thanks to my ace advisor, patient coach, and resolutely determined "book shepherd" Claudia Gere. This lamb would have lost its way long ago, if not for your steady guidance. It was an arduous passage, I only crossed because of your patient assurance, calming influence, and well placed pushes to keep me moving forward.

Many thanks as well to Claudia's second in command, and my "editor in chief," Brent Allard. There isn't a sentence in this book that escaped your sharp eye for detail, and many were much improved by your input. Plus you pulled off the equivalent of a literary ventriloquist act by simultaneously correcting my words without changing my voice.

I'm deeply grateful to my friend and shining example, Dan Burrus for writing this book's foreword and imbuing it with his keen intellect and highly developed "flash foresight."

My warm appreciation to photography angels: Jeff Boudro, Stephanie Oates, Wes Page, Dov Friedman, Jazmine Peck, and Jeannette Tokarz; the photographs that enliven these pages and back cover are both the fruits and the proofs of your artistry.

I thank my lucky stars to belong to both a great performing arts guild and a wonderful creative writing group.

In ways too mysterious to recount, this book got birthed because of John Porcino, Amy Swisher, Sid Simon, Marianne Simon, Tom Lehman, Mark Summa, Chris Yerlig, Henry Lappen, Robert Rivest, Tim Van Egmund, and Trevor the Games Man.

And speaking of artists, I want to give a warm hand to Illustrator, David Costello for creating the supple hands, colorful balls, and catchy lettering that brighten the cover.

A big THANKS as well to Chris Reagan, president of GetAheadPro Speaker's Bureau for being my best business partner, patiently walking me through my first webinar, and being in my corner—creatively collaborating with me every step of the way.

Last, this book wouldn't be in your hands without the encouragement I got to write it from my National Speaker's Association friends and mentors. I feel fortunate to have such savvy "friendtors" and send a special shout out to: Dr. Tony Campolo, Dr. Terry Paulson, Chris Clarke Epstein, Steve Saffron, Dan Thurmon, Dr. Janet Lappe, Stephen Shapiro, Patrick Donadio, Marilee Driscoll, Dr. Alan Zimmerman, Shep Hyken, and Marjorie Brody (and an even longer list of "honorable mentions": David Glickman, Alan Berg, Giovanni Livera, Dr Dennis Reina, Alan Hunkins, Mike Robbins, Theo Androus, Lou Heckler, Mike McKinley, Jim Cathcart, Eric Chester, Jon Wee, Owen Morse, Tim O'Shea, Greg Godek... plus my dance partners: Diane Ripstein, Lynn Durham, Rochelle Rice, June Cline, and Monique Bourgeois).

And to so many others, I've met along the way, too numerous to mention, who helped me along this path.

Here's the Gist

(CliffsNotes for Those Who Like a Shortcut)

It's a juggle out there, and the speed we need to toss and catch is clearly accelerating. What isn't so clear is how to keep pace in a way that is exhilarating, not exhausting. Change is a constant, and coping with constant change is a daunting challenge. Trying to keep abreast is like trying to keep all the balls in the air; an imbalancing act that leaves many of us chronically overwhelmed and under-slept. Literally, and figuratively, good jugglers know how to catch a lot of balls simultaneously. Great jugglers know how to let go of everything nonessential. They recognize that a DROP is a "daily reminder of patience," and a "dramatic rejection of perfection." Both of which keep them from tossing in their sleep!

This small book summarizes three large lessons from the craft of juggling that lead to better life balance and inner contentment. It lays no claim to being the definitive authority on the subject. It does take solace in the idea that the concept of mind-body harmony originated in Greece (so, no wonder it's often Greek to me!). Part One takes its cue from the Oracle at Delphi, "Know thyself. Nothing to excess."

Lesson One: *Finding a rhythm that works best for your biology, and your biography, is a pivotal priority.* The founder of

Taoism, Lao Tzu, nailed it when he wrote, "Timing is the root of all grace."

Lesson Two: *The ruin of peace is perfectionism.* Worry doesn't solve anything, but it can overcomplicate everything! The key to leveraging our personal and professional effectiveness, is to recognize what areas we can and can't influence and focus within the locus of our control. In life, as in juggling, the best way to ensure accuracy is to take careful aim.

Lesson Three: *There's a thin line between racing and chasing.* In the marketplace, speed sells and speed thrills. In our private lives, speed stresses and speed kills our vital need for serenity. The race may go to the swift, but the chase can quickly shift from skillful acceleration to a sad illustration of how "haste makes waste." The beauty of a good juggling act, or any graceful activity, happens because performers know how to take their time. Key transitions aren't rushed. Instead they are handled so smoothly the performers make it look easy. They've learned the core Zen practice of shifting from powerful effort to effortless power.

It's hardly possible to succeed in business without embracing the old truism that "time is money." It's impossible to have a healthy personal life without leisure. The people who do well professionally, and personally, wisely recognize that downtime is found money; a chance to relax, a moment to pause and reflect, providing vital replenishment. These are the times when the balls are hanging in the air like the spaces between the notes in a beautifully composed symphony. These rests complement the rhythm and are the still points of silence that enhance the score.

This book takes traditional opposites, like concentration and relaxation, and integrates them through the concept of flow.

Part One reveals the primary obstacles to being an easy-flowing person are excessive worrying and failing to keep problems in perspective. It summarizes core concepts of life balance, and provides several original tools and techniques for maintaining perspective in the midst of a challenging situation. Aphorisms like, "Don't complain, reframe," and "Pits are also seeds," encourage readers to develop their inner R&R (resiliency and resourcefulness).

Part Two focuses on how to cope with constant change and still stay sane." With humor and heart it shares true stories of how to shift from "Oh hell!" to "Oh well." It's laced with inspiring examples of people who tapped their childlike imagination to counterbalance a heavy concern with a light curiosity. It also provides several common sense practices that deepen our capacities to refresh, recharge, and revitalize using guided meditation practices adapted from the teaching of Buddhist monk Thich Nhat Hanh. This rich, inner wisdom of the East is reinforced by pragmatic Western principles gleaned from Stephen Covey's landmark classic, *The Seven Habits of Highly Effective People*.

Throughout are original ideas and insights inspired by nature in general and waterfalls in particular. Acronyms like WHOOPS (when humans overcome obstacles, Providence smiles), and OHIO (only handle it once), as opposed to MISSISSIPPI (maybe I should save it since someday it'll perhaps prove important), provide an even mix of humor and hope.

Part Three synthesizes key elements of time management and stress reduction into a hybrid I call Kind Management. It tackles two closely related modern *sin*-dromes, overwork and overload, causing us to be chronically under-slept. It reveals that the two main culprits share the same root cause: a gnawing feeling of uncertainty. "How can I keep all these balls in the air at once? How can I pull all the pieces together (with so little time, money, or support)?" Sound familiar?

Developing a practice of kindfulness deepens our capacity for self-care. The more consciously aware we are of our most pressing needs, the better we're able to envision what we need to resolve them. Figuring out where and how we want to finish removes a layer of doubt that otherwise sits on us like a big chunk of deadweight.

No good jugglers begin a balancing act with a sharp machete, a flaming torch, and a big ol' bowling ball without knowing where all three are going to end up. (This also greatly reduces the likelihood that they catch the right end of the first two dangerous objects and the latter doesn't land on their nose!)

Fortunately, once we've got a clear bead on where we're headed, our mental MapQuest quickly begins to supply directions and sort out the best route. Clarifying our intent informs our priorities and provides the scaffolding that guides completion. Intentions become imperatives. We push aside external distractions, push through internal divisions, and focus full attention on their successful completion. (Go team, go!)

In sum, Kind Management is a form of personal insurance that replaces the need for urgent care with relaxed self-caring. Practicing *kindfulness* allows us to align our deeds and our creeds in a way that's guided by an inner compass, rather than an external clock. Part Three concludes with a detailed list of small, daily rituals of renewal that help us get out of our heads, or at least out of the house, reviving both our energy and our outlook. (Amen.)

PART ONE

What...Who... Me, Worry?

Who ever thought up the word "mammogram?"
Every time I hear it, I think I'm supposed to put my breast in an
envelope and send it to someone.
~ Jan King

How to Have Less Stress & More Zest

Some days I'm so frazzled I wish could look up everything I'm confounded about in a Zen dictionary. I imagine somewhere there's a slender, beautifully bound volume with a simple black and white cover that contains a single word. One word whose definition instantly dissolves all my quandaries; wór•ry, *verb*: the vain attempt to repair broken wind.

I'm still searching for that book. To date, it looks like that dictionary's only going to exist if I write it, and I'm not that Zen! Fortunately, I'm not always that frazzled either. At my best, I avoid the rabbit hole of worry and concentrate on what's within my circle of influence. Once I stop fixating on things that are outside my control, I start focusing on constructive alternatives. One of my favorites is to take something that's bothering me and reconsider it from a neutral viewpoint. The minute I do that, something in my head shifts and transforms concern into curiosity — *presto!* The problem stops eating me up and starts leading me down a path of discovery.

Emotionally, I switch from feeling cursed to feeling challenged. Trust me, the latter is a lot better headspace than the former! Once my brain shifts from irritation to intrigue, the issue takes on a whole different quality. Instead of an annoying impediment, it evolves into an interesting puzzle that my mind becomes increasingly committed to solving. Sure enough, once I stop lamenting about feeling stuck and start focusing on finding missing pieces, I see a bigger picture. The more puzzle parts there are, the more fun the process is of getting them to fit together.

Which reminds me of an apt joke where two guys walk into a bar (now there's a shocking set up!). They walk up to the bartender, plop a jigsaw puzzle on the counter, and shout triumphantly, "We did it! Drinks on the house!"

The bartender says, "Congratulations," and pours a round for everyone. Then he picks up the puzzle and peers at the cover picture of a cowboy. "This is what you put together?"

The guys hoist their beers. "Yeah, we did it inside of thirty minutes tops!" The patrons beside them clink their glasses in a toast.

The bartender is underwhelmed. "I don't get it, what's so hard about assembling a simple puzzle of a cowboy?"

The guys grin back. "Wasn't hard nohow, we done it in less than half an hour."

The bartender stares back incredulously, and says, "Doing that puzzle inside of thirty minutes warrants a celebration?"

The guys point proudly at the side of the box and gleefully reply, "Sure does. Says there three-to-five years!"

Chapter 1

Cope with Constant Change
& Still Stay Sane

Inspiration

The latest statistics show that 150 people die every year from being hit by falling coconuts. Not to worry, drug makers are developing a vaccine.

~ Jim Carrey

Photograph by Wes Page

Insight

Change is unsettling. At its best, it breaks us out of a rut and reshapes our perception. Occasionally, we instantly recognize the benefits of doing something differently and adapt immediately. More often, it takes awhile for us to come around. We've got to adjust our stance several times before we see the shift in a positive light.

Change is a disruption from routine. Most of us are initially reluctant to let go of what's familiar. As much as we know, intellectually, that venturing outside our comfort zone is essential for growth, emotionally the fear of the unknown is a pervasive shackle and pernicious barrier.

Change is both a challenge and a catalyst. When we're dealing with the unknown most of us have a knee-jerk reaction that says, "This stinks!" But what if instead we said, "This stretches"? Saying something stinks predisposes us to grimace and groan. Seeing it as a stretch primes us to extend and grow. Change our words, change our world!

Change isn't easy, but whenever we have the courage to walk through the doorway of discomfort, we deepen our capacity for growth. Uncertainty sucks! But it also draws out our character and is the only true testing ground for faith. In the memorable words of Mark Twain, "There's a reason to go out on a limb, that's where the fruit is." Change the lens we look through, change the life we lead.

Change is a constant, so is choice. We can choose to feel persecuted and put upon in a way that predisposes us to feel pessimistic. Or we can look through a more positive lens, and be proactive and optimistic. The former is a recipe for a lifetime of resentment and resignation. The latter is a powerful prescription for resiliency and resourcefulness.

(Hint: Take the latter. You'll be a lot more popular at parties, and more importantly, you'll like your own company a lot better too!)

The saying, "Shit happens," is a handy reminder that change can be seen as crap or compost. Prolific author Brian Tracey wisely observed, "Difficulties are placed in our path not to obstruct, but to instruct." During a time of difficult change it sure helps to realize that we're not just laboring, we're learning. Luckily, in most cases, what feels like crap at the time turns out to be potent fertilizer down the line. I know for a fact; some of my toughest transitions, including a marital separation that's gotta go down in the Guinness Book of Worst Divorces, forced me and my child down an arduous path that led to a much healthier, and a whole lot more peaceful household.

Change is an equal opportunity destroyer; no one is immune. No matter who you are, sometimes in life you reap the fruit, and other times you eat the pits. But as lousy as change can feel in the moment, more often than not, our most troubled times prove the antecedents to some of our most treasured attributes: humility, compassion, patience, courage, and empathy. And for heaven's sake, let's not forget the best silver lining of weathering a stormy time is that somewhere down the line it turns into great fodder for a funny story! (The next chapter being a rollicking example.)

I don't know if there's a psychological classification for people who keep trying to deny, or turn a blind eye, to the things they need to shift. But I'm sure if they come up with a therapy that treats being change-averse as an addiction, someone will come up with a catchy name like Avoiders Anonymous. Of course, to ensure it deviated from the status quo, and fostered receptivity to novelty, it would have to be a thirteen-step program. I'm guessing its version of the Serenity Prayer would go something like, "Grant me the wisdom to broadly cooperate with the unavoidable, the courage to boldly counter the unacceptable, and the wisdom to blithely take a pass on the inevitable!"

It's a grand irony, but change is here to stay. Bottom line: it's a part of being human that's never going to go away. As the *Star Trek* saying goes, "Resistance is futile." So, instead of being reluctant, let's be receptive to rolling with whatever life throws at us. When it looks like the changes are obstructing, uncover what they're instructing. In short, don't complain, reframe. And remember, no matter how much it may feel like the pits, on some level, pits are also seeds!

Intent

Today I am trusting that the changes, which seem like the pits, are actually the seeds to a surprisingly positive development.

Introspection

What did you learn the hard way that turned out to be an unexpected gift?

Who helps you believe in your ability to bounce back from adversity?

How can you help others manage change more calmly?

Implementation

The minute I put this book down, I'm going to pick up the phone and thank _____ for being such a good ally.

Chapter 2

Leaping to Confusion

Inspiration

If you see the world in black and white, you're missing important grey matter!

~ Jack Fyock

Photograph by Stephanie Oates

Insight

According to Dr. Bernie Siegel, in the year he spent as an "outside observer on the Board of Directors for Heaven," the following was the most frequently asked question upon arrival at the pearly gates: "Good lord, why was I so serious back there?" Meanwhile, to date, the most frequent question asked on Earth is, "Where's the bathroom?"

For most earthlings, anxious confusion causes the equivalent of emotional constipation. Our feelings get so bound up by worry, our coping skills get blocked. A minor concern, which in a calmer mood would be an inconvenience, becomes a major catastrophe. Apropos, here's a humorous example of how high stress sparks our brains to burst into calamitous conclusions. It comes from a story my fellow motivational speaker, Glenna Salsbury, found in an article published by the Associated Press, but with a few embellishments (because hey, how else can I get my poetic license recertified!).

On a broiling August afternoon, a shopping mall security guard was out making his obligatory parking lot rounds. Sweating profusely in his tight uniform, the guard is stunned to discover a driver in a parked car, with the engine off, and all the windows rolled up. Confused and already a trifle concerned, the guard ventures closer to the car and sees a middle-aged woman with her fingers laced against the back of her skull, her face wincing in pain. "Ma'am," he asks in a tone of alarm, tapping on the driver's side window, "Are you alright?" Holding her hands pressed tightly against her head the woman answers without turning her neck, "No, I've been shot!"

Instantly, the guard pulls the door handle but it's locked. He looks at the woman imploringly and says, "It's OK to let me in Ma'am, I'm a security guard." Motionless, the woman replies, "I can't move my hands. My brains are leaking out, and I've got to hold them in."

Desperate to help, the guard uses a locksmith tool, opens the door, and discovers a trail of sticky bread dough dripping down the driver's neck. A quick investigation reveals the woman had left a bag of groceries in the back seat while she shopped. When she returned a couple hours later and got behind the wheel, a canister of Pepperidge Farm Crescent Rolls baking in the extreme heat exploded, rocketing a wad of dough smack into the back of her scalp!

Jumping to the unmistakable conclusion that she'd been shot by an unseen assassin, the woman then mistook the oozing dough for her brains. Instantly, she interlocked both hands in a desperate attempt to keep them in. And given how quickly the brain cells she had to begin with leaped to confusion, it's easy to understand why she was so afraid to lose any additional amount!

Luckily, once the guard got her out of the car and showed her the canister, she realized she was unharmed, and the only further explosion was a loud cackle of shared laughter. Which, as explosions go, is definitely the best way to turn every day into a joyful Fourth of July holiday!

Intent

Today instead of jumping to catastrophes, I'm celebrating the freedom to use poetic license to link humorous misperceptions like a string of spiritual firecrackers.

Introspection

When was the last time you overreacted?

Had you stayed calm, what unnecessary stress could have been avoided?

What is your best coping strategy for turning stumbling blocks into stepping stones?

Implementation

Remember: *If you write it, you invite it.*

To leverage what I learned, my to-do for today is:

Here are two action steps I will accomplish this week:
1)

2)

Chapter 3

Outlook Is an Inside Job

Inspiration

Perspective is worth 80 IQ points.
~ Alan Kay

Photograph by Jeannette Tokarz

Insight

It's a juggle out there, and challenges come at us left and right. I believe the bulk of our stress comes in two sizes: overwhelm and overwrought. Most of us are all too familiar with the first; the feeling of having too many big things to deal with all at once. Overwrought is the opposite. It's making too big a deal of just one thing. The bad news is, when you're the one who's confusing a small calamity for a sizable catastrophe (like the woman who mistook an exploding canister of Pepperidge Farm Crescent Rolls for an unseen assailant's gunshot), you're the last to know.

The good news is that even when we're so wrapped around the axle and we're in danger of getting dragged under it, there is a way to prevent ourselves from getting sunk. In the grand tradition of teaching what *I* most need to learn, here's my method for making sure I don't turn a minor setback into a major misfortune.

To start, mentally step back and emotionally disengage from the sense of urgency. The goal is to get your mind on higher ground where no immediate action or decision is required. Happily, the minute action no longer feels imminent, my whole thought process seems to simultaneously slow, and calm down.

Once you see a broader view, the next step is to envision that your brain comes with the equivalent of a built-in camera that has five adjustable lenses. For reasons, which will rapidly become obvious, my term for this technique is the *5X5 Viewshifter*. Each lens is a perspective-shifting question that widens your view from as close a time frame as five hours to as far away as five years. Here's how it works.

Pick a problem, any problem (I sound like a magician fanning out a deck of cards), preferably one that's a real pain in the rear. Once you've identified the irritant, you're ready to use the camera. The first lens stop is to simply ask yourself, how big a deal will this be five hours from now? In most cases, five hours isn't enough time to create any additional composure, but it gives us a small start towards lifting our nose off the grindstone. Anything that gets the problem to stop pressing down on us so hard, helps us see a little bigger picture.

The second adjustable lens shift is to ask, how big a deal will this be five days from now? Personally, I've been amazed at how something that seemed monumental on Monday somehow becomes a whole lot more manageable by Friday. Sometimes just being able to push a problem out to the end of the week gives us the distance we need to put it in proper perspective.

And if five days later isn't enough space, I'm sure you can guess where the next two lens stops are going: how big a deal will this be in five weeks... in five months? Short of a serious medical condition, or a true emotional tragedy, when we can view what's bothering us from a vantage point of more than a month later, or almost half a year down the road, the issue ceases to loom so large. Instead of feeling panic, we see that "this too shall pass." The awareness that what's troubling us isn't permanent, and one day will be water over the dam, buoys our spirits and builds the confidence that we're going to get past this. Heck, with any luck, one day we'll even look back at it and laugh!

On rare occasions, we're dealing with something so devastating we need to pull out the fifth lens shift: how big a deal will this be in five years? It took me almost that long to get over the emotional and financial fallout from my divorce. But now I can look back on that dismal period as growing pains that nurtured my capacity to be a good partner. Five years later, I got a whole new lease on life, and today I'm in a healthy, committed relationship, and my daughter, who I was so worried about at the time, has turned out much the wiser (and putting those smarts to good use at Smith College!).

So, that's the 5X5 Viewshifter: an easy to remember, simple to apply technique that progressively expands your perspective, extends your ability to stay centered, and all but eliminates confusing dripping bread dough for oozing brain cells! It's not rocket science, but it is a pragmatic tool that provides an instant injunction from jumping to false conclusions. Try it, you'll like it. And with any luck, it'll soon become a tried and true technique for keeping a balanced view. I know firsthand, it's a common sense practice that really works (when I calm down enough to actually employ it!).

Intent

Today I am widening my view and broadening my horizons in a way that turns millstones into stepping stones.

Introspection

When did you have a situation where you blew something out of proportion?

What did you learn from it that lets you be more likely to keep things in perspective?

How could you integrate the 5X5 Viewshifter technique in a way that would enhance your capacity to deal with overload and feel less overwhelmed?

Implementation

Remember: *What you focus on, you feed.*

Here's the main thing I'm taking away (and taking action on) today:

My game plan this week is to make these promises to myself come true:
1)

2)

Chapter 4

From Peeved to Poised

Inspiration

When someone is impatient and says, "I haven't got all day," I always wonder, "What hours are you missing? How can you not have all day?"

~ George Carlin

Photograph by Jeff Boudro

Insight

When I'm running late for an appointment, and the car in front of me is driving like a slow turkey, two phrases vie for expression: "Oh hell!" and "Oh well." Both are short and are spelled identically, save for one lone letter. But somehow that small difference can have a surprisingly large consequence.

"Oh hell!" predisposes me to feel perturbed and act like I'm oppressed. "Oh well," helps me stay calm and remain buoyant. True to its namesake, "Oh hell!" makes me get hot under the collar; I sweat and fret and want to hold up the bottom three fingers on my right hand, and shout at the slow driver, "Read between the lines!"

By happy contrast, responding, "Oh well," eases my haste and eliminates my irritability. It's as if the very word *well*, evokes a quality of wellness that allows me to accept and adapt. Instead of fueling frustration, it primes my mental pump to come up with contingencies. Rather than flip the bird, I flick on the car's CD player, and slip in the audiobook that I just remembered has a perfect joke to offset being late for my meeting: "The past, the present, and the future all walk into a bar. Instantly the mood in the place turned tense!"

Sometimes life goes swimmingly, and a break in our schedule even allows us to get in a swim. At our best, we can eschew the damnation of "Oh hell!" by viewing what's gone awry as the equivalent of the ceremonial broken glass at a Jewish wedding. Note to readers, I'm Jewish by birth, but my upbringing wasn't exactly religious. My neighborhood had families where children were raised Orthodox, Conservative, or Reformed. My family? Reupholstered! Hence, I lay no claim to scholarly accuracy about Jewish wedding lore. However, after witnessing several traditional ceremonies, I began to think there was a very pragmatic reason behind the ritual of deliberately stomping on a wine glass. The rationale being that anytime human beings try to stage a complex event, something's bound to go wrong. So, *nooo*? Why not work fallibility right into the ceremony? Break a glass and chalk it up to, "Oh well, something is bound to go amiss, better it be this than some true calamity."

Over time, this way of looking at snafus morphed into a kind of faith. When things don't go according to plan, it's because what's transpiring is actually part of a much bigger plan that I'm not privy to. I don't understand how or why it works, but I trust the universe knows what it's doing. My friend John Porcino is such a true believer in Providence that the other day when he stepped into a boiling hot car, his reaction was, "Oh well. Looks like I'll get to take that sauna I was hoping for after all!"

Inspired by my friend, I found a similarly positive way to frame a small misfortune that occurred in the community recreation center's large outdoor pool. It was a blazing afternoon. After diving in and swimming a lap of crawl, I switched to the backstroke. Closing my eyes to block out the sun, I glided serenely across the water and barreled my head smack into the back wall. My eyes burst open. "I've been shot!" I'm kidding of course, and my wide-eyed stare quickly confirmed the pool hid neither assassins nor explosive Pepperidge Farm canisters. Still, I leaped out of the pool and gingerly felt my head for a bump, or worse, blood. Finding none, I looked up at the clouds and said, "Oh well.

Thanks universe, just what I needed: a quick chiropractic adjustment and at no extra charge!"

Intent

Today I'm trusting that whatever goes awry will just make my brain more adaptable and my body more durable!

Introspection

In what way does "Oh well," resonate the most for you?

How could you react differently to avoid "Oh hell!" in a way that helps you feel less overwhelmed?

Who is a walking inspiration when it comes to being faithful in Providence and flexible about people?

Why would it be wise to tell them so, and for extra credit, ask for their assistance?

Implementation

Remember: *What you elucidate, you cultivate.*

At least one time today I will:

This week I will take these two simple steps to stay calm and feel more rested:
1)

2)

Chapter 5

The Wisdom of the Waterfalls

Inspiration

I would love to live like a river flows, carried by the surprise of its own unfolding.

~ John Donohue, "Fluent"

Photograph by Stephanie Oates

Insight

What is it about waterfalls? Why do they send such a soothing signal to my psyche? How do they blend sight and sound so seamlessly that they become both fluid artwork and mobile music? Where is the secret of their strength to cleave solid rock and the source of their simplicity to pick the path of least resistance? What better exemplifies relaxed fluidity and epitomizes graceful surrender?

I neither comprehend the complexities of these questions nor crave the answers. I claim no expertise in explaining why waterfalls are harmony in motion. I'm content to simply sit back and welcome the water's shining inspiration for reflection.

Hey, how can you see a stream slide down a mountain and not marvel at its mellifluousness? To me, the rhythmic rushing of a river over rocks is a soundtrack for spiritual equanimity.

Walk along the river, sweet lullaby. It just keeps on flowin'; it don't worry where it's goin'.
~ Allman Brothers Band, "Blue Sky"

For my music, waterfalls mystically blend structure and spontaneity. The banks provide a solid container, the tumbling waters wantonly meander; one part a jazz drummer like Philly Joe Jones providing a steady backbeat, one part a vocalist like Ella Fitzgerald scat singing at The Cotton Club in Harlem. Winding around boulders and cleaving through crevices, the rocks and the river gracefully interweave, the rushing current twisting the stream into liquid braids of play, power, and peace.

OK, Peck, enough poetry, get to the practical part (oh alright, alter ego, if you insist). Cascades are both inspirational and instructive. The water flows because it goes with gravity. Rather than resist the rock's hard barrier, the current winds its way around it.

Lesson One: *Why force when you can flow?* Progress results more readily when we relax and allow events to evolve and ourselves to unfold at an unhurried pace. Rather than press and strain, my mood becomes a lot less stressed when I invoke this simple credo: "Let it go, and ease the woe. Take it slow, and trust you'll know when to reap and where to sow."

Waterfalls are never the same. They vary by season and volume of precipitation. When the rain pours, and the water pounds, the river races. When the skies stay sunny and a dry spell sets in, the current strolls a slow, serpentine path.

Lesson Two: *Go with what you got.* Success stems more from fluidity and flexibility than from fixed agendas and rigidity. Take it as it comes and enjoy the ride. When dark clouds gather, remember, the silver lining of a rainstorm is it gives waterfalls license to reign in their full glory. The only way a brook or stream becomes a cascade is when something challenges its momentum. Without rocks it remains a river. No resistance, no running water, and no rising to the sound of liquid music worthy of the name *waterfalls.*

(Bonus) Lesson Three: *Impediments fuel ingenuity.* It's the challenge of circumventing barriers that compels the river to constantly reinvent itself. It's nature's version of the WHOOPS factor (when humans overcome obstacles, Providence smiles).

Intent

Today I'm living my life the way water flows down a gentle hillside: rhythmically, resiliently, and resourcefully.

Introspection

When was the last time you listened to a waterfall?

What impact would it have on a key relationship if you viewed problems as rocks fueling resiliency and resourcefulness?

How can you work free of a barrier by finding a way to flow around it?

Why would doing so increase your ingenuity and improve your capacity to cope with overload?

Implementation

Remember: *If you write it, you invite it.*

This is the week when I:

To be sure I leverage what I just learned, here are two lessons I'm going to put into practice:
1)

2)

PART TWO

Laugh, Learn, & Think Long-Term

Freedom is the oxygen of the soul.
~ Moshe Dayan

As long as the world is turning and spinning,
we're gonna be dizzy, and we're gonna make mistakes.
~ Mel Brooks

How to Stop Sprinting & Start Strolling

When I was a boy, back in the Paleolithic period of home entertainment, I loved an LP recording of the vintage comedy routine where Carl Reiner interviewed a Mel Brooks character called the "2000-Year-Old Man." One of my favorite lines was this response to Reiner's question about the secret of his longevity: "I never rush. Never run for a bus; there'll always be another. I just stroll jaunty n' jolly. That's mine peppy ways!"

In sad contrast, at society's current frenetic pace, staying at the top of our profession pressures us to compress tasks the way computers compress data. Heaven help humanity if there is a link between leisure and longevity. Because at the rate the digital revolution is escalating, the more smart product time savers we buy, the less serene moments we have. Tranquility is in serious decline and burnout is rapidly on the rise.

It's a juggle out there, and coping with constant change is a daily demand. Trying to stay sane while working faster and faster, running from one task to the next, and the next, and the next, and the… is exhausting. This is why *Part Two* is all about finding ways to reverse the do-everything-electronic current, and remove ourselves from the 24/7 rat race. It doesn't offer any magic bullet, but it does provide several common sense practices that deepen our capacities to refresh, recharge, and revitalize.

Chapter 6

Multitasking, Multitracking, Mucho-Taxing!

Inspiration

In love, somehow, a man's heart is always either exceeding the speed limit or getting parked in the wrong place.
~ Helen Rowland

Photograph by Stephanie Oates

Insight

This chapter tackles two closely related modern *sindromes*: overload and overwhelm. Here's hoping it shines some light or at least sheds some stress!

The Internet is like a giant, high-tech recording studio. Thoughts reverberate in quadrophonic sound, ideas are instantly digitized, and caution is overdubbed. Immediacy is prized, while patience is a virtue the virtual world has rarely recognized. Pop-ups screen out everything that's not urgent: iPhone screens, YouTube screens, Wii screens. Our brains scream, "Too many screens!"

Between Web 2.0, 3.0, 4.0, and nonstop social media, my mind is in perpetual overload mode. My mental wires are so overheated, my cerebral circuits are fried. ("That's it, I'm pulling the plug!") Trouble is, my psyche's so accustomed to being surrounded by stimuli, silence is strangely disquieting. Even the term *downtime* makes me doubt I'll ever rise to the level I aspire to achieve. Taking time for leisure is like paddling the mainstream against the current. Downtime means I'm not keeping up. Going offline is going against the flow of oncoming traffic. Disconnecting feels like I'm endangering my social media survival.

OK, so maybe I can't just pull the plug. Still there's got to be some way to hit the reset button. Some psychic release valve that frees me from feeling so stressed about supper being late that I stop shouting, "Faster! Faster, you fool!" to the microwave. *Hmmm…* maybe it's time for me to take a page from my own presentation and practice what I preach about: the fact that pits are also seeds.

In hopes that necessity will once again birth invention and help me cook up a creative solution, here's a fast stab at Rob's Reset Recipe.

Rule One: *Work backwards.* Focus on the end results first and let the starting points fall into place. I've learned, in most cases, the root cause of overwhelm is uncertainty. "How can I pull all these pieces together (with so little time, money, support, etc.)?" Sound familiar? Figuring out where and how we want to finish removes a layer of doubt that otherwise sits on us like a big chunk of deadweight. Once we have a clear bead on where we're headed, our built-in mental MapQuest quickly begins to supply directions and sort out the best route. Clarifying our intent informs our priorities and provides the scaffolding that guides completion; intentions become imperatives. We push aside external distractions, push through internal divisions, and focus full attention to their completion.

Rule Two: *Watch your language.* The words we speak to others, and especially the ones we say to ourselves, about our workload profoundly impact our perceptions and attitudes. "I'm so busy today I don't have time to breathe!" is a blueprint for a big, brick, stress-and-strain duplex right on the main drag in Overload Land. By contrast, saying aloud or internally, "I'm being sure to budget into my busy day some time to unwind and recharge my battery," signals a mind-set of healthy self-care. Bottom line: beliefs drive behaviors. By finding one that links recreation with reconnection, we ensure small daily rituals of renewal like a fifteen-minute walk in nature, or playing a couple tunes with a pal. Anything that gets you out of your head and into your heart, revives your energy and revitalizes your outlook.

Rule Three: *Pace thyself.* Give your brain a break. When our minds are in hyper-drive worrying about the future, and our thoughts are whirring nowhere fast, it's time to unplug. Step outdoors and go somewhere slow. I know, I know, with all the tasks on your to-do list (never mind your didn't-do list!), it's hard to stay a human being and not become a human *doing*: a busybody consumed by laptop computers or tethered to portable wireless devices.

It's not easy to unhook and unwind. Media blares in our ears and eyes around the clock, but our cerebral circuitry isn't designed to work 24/7. Whatever we read about mental health might as well be a myth, if we never put our internal hard drive on hibernate. It may sound old fashioned, but the best way to be present is still to do so in person. Our heads connect better to our hearts when we're offline and experience real-time interactions face-to-face.

In sum, laptops and smartphones are modern marvels, but there's nothing antiquated about putting down the iPhone and making eye contact. The fewer things there are in the way, the easier it is for two human beings to feel close. We are social creatures who crave tactile connection from the moment we're born. It's a healthy instinct to want to feel warmly connected to another human being. Which is why, when it comes to showing affection, I'll take skin touch over touch screens anytime!

Intent

Today I am monitoring my screen time, and maintaining a healthy balance between human viewing and human being.

Introspection

Why is starting with the end in mind such a vital prerequisite for productivity?

How can you combine an important belief with a weekly behavior to revitalize your spirit?

Who is the first face you think of when you picture spending quality time offline, face-to-face, and heart-to-heart?

Implementation

Remember: *What you elucidate, you cultivate.*

Before today is over, I commit to carving out space in my schedule to be offline and connect in real time with _____.

At least twice this week, I vow to do these two things to stay more present:
1)

2)

Chapter 7

Off the Clock &
In the Moment

Inspiration

You know you're stressed, when you're in such a rush to get dressed, you try to pull your pants on over your head!
~ Paraphrase of Woody Allen quip

Photograph by Wes Page

Insight

Back in the sixties, signs said, "Speed Kills!" Today all signs indicate that speed sells: rapid transit, fast food, flash drives, instant anything, and electronic everything. Our cultural fascination with acceleration parallels the media's infatuation with innovation. Time-compressing, cutting-edge features are the chief appeal in advertisements for the latest techno products (whose success rates, at inculcation, breed a virtual fixation).

For all the hype about smart devices that let us do more in less time, the bottom line is, shortcuts can short circuit intimacy. It's a juggle out there because the quicker products can microcompute, the more massively the communication overload in our lives increases. Time savers are wonderful inventions, but the constant pressure of having to think and do everything faster, and faster, *and faster* is a major source of stress.

Clearly, rushing isn't conducive to good self-care. Rapidly accomplishing one task after another may increase our daily output; it sure doesn't do much for our inner contentment. Keeping up a frantic pace is a high price for lowering our moments of peace. On the surface, doing things quicker and getting more done is efficient, but ineffective stress management, racing, and relaxing don't mix.

Sometimes we need to take ourselves off the treadmill, periodically step out of the mainstream, spread a towel on the bank, and bask in the mental sunshine of a brief respite; a few minutes where we can be in the moment and off the clock.

Nature never feels pressured to increase the rate the sun rises or sets. So, why don't we schedule our days more naturally? Imagine, if despite the external pressures to speed up, we internally cultivated a love for all things seasoned. Here's my idea of a go-slow spree: the top ten reasons why downshifting our daily schedules from sprint to stroll is a boon for our overall wellness.

Number Ten: *Give our brains a break!* Instead of feeling pressured to put in hours of speed screen reading we get to unplug, pick up a good book, and slowly savor the simple pleasure of reading for pure enjoyment.

Number Nine: *Give our bodies a break!* Quit obsessing about cellulite and receding hairlines, and bring back recess and quiet hour. (Cookies and milk aren't just for kids!)

Number Eight: *Break the routine and turn it into a ritual of renewal.* Instead of a twenty-minute power nap, why not treat ourselves to a leisurely siesta? (And while we're at it, substitute our standard quick rinse in the shower with a luxurious soak in a tub.)

Number Seven: *Eschew the expressway for the scenic route.* Rather than racing to our destination, we roll along and enjoy the ride. No more gripping the wheel with the car stereo pounding out hard driving music. Now we sit back comfortably in our seat and listen to stress-soothing melodies. (Who needs Bad Company and Talking Heads when you can relax to Buffet and Brahms?)

Number Six: *Log off and lay on the veranda.* Make leisure less about social media online, and more about real-time social bonding through shared stories and true two-way conversations.

Number Five: *Swap high-speed modems for slow-paced mentoring.* Instead of frenetically trying to keep pace with accelerated e-learning, let's spend some quality time patiently passing along our life lessons. (Which brings a whole new meaning to hearing someone "live and in person.")

Number Four: *Don't take out, dine in!* Forgo fast food in favor of making and enjoying a home cooked meal. (No one has to pick up the check and nobody needs to leave a tip!)

Number Three: *Eat wisely and eat well.* Change our allegiance from the unholy alliance of frozen entrees and microwave ovens, to a healthy reliance on local farmers markets and organic produce.

Number Two: *Easy does it.* Rather than rush to get to work on time, our *work* is to take our time and spend it lavishly on, and with, our loved ones. (*Nuff* said!)

And the top reason why downshifting our daily schedules from sprint to stroll is a boon for our overall wellness?

Number One: *Replace the need for urgent care with relaxed self-caring.* Forget long lists and manic multitasking. Let's designate an afternoon to focus on getting one task done well and calling it a day. (And if anyone stays later or does something longer, it's only because they're choosing to play overtime.)

Intent

Today I'm letting go of the left lane, exiting the highway, and contently taking the long way home (maybe even stopping off to surprise a friend).

Introspection

When, and where, in your day would giving yourself a short break have the biggest impact?

What does taking the scenic route mean you would do differently?

How would increased self-care help you sleep more deeply and arise more refreshed?

Implementation

Remember: *What you articulate, you cultivate.*

To be sure I leverage what I just learned, here are two lessons I'm going to put into practice:

1)

2)

This is the week when I:

Chapter 8

Slow Listener, Fast Learner

Inspiration

The only problem with the speed of light is it gets here too early in the morning!

~ Danny Neaverth

Photograph by Wes Page

Insight

It sucks to be a slow learner in a rapid-fire culture. From the college classroom to the corporate boardroom, the focal points are the same: accelerate your learning curve, increase your earning capacity. Don't get me wrong, I have no beef with being a fast learner. I strive to be a quick study, and I thrive when I can swiftly process the problem and provide a lightning solution.

I'm all for soaking up pertinent information like the proverbial sponge. It's the wringing out part that perturbs me. The pace of my plugged-in, hyper-driven life is already so squeezed my spirit is starting to shrivel. I get that the race belongs to the swift, and the first product to the marketplace fetches the best price. Still, I hunger for an inner fulfillment that goes beyond being the first to cross the finish line.

I don't want to experience a midlife crisis. I want a long life sense of calm. A quiet assurance that lets me step off the beaten path; a pause to take stock of my core priorities; a time to pull together the key threads and fashion a plan for the future. A life strategy that's less fixated on increased income and revenues, and more focused on lasting outcomes and loving relationships.

I've learned I allow this strategy to develop best when I devote time to deepening the trust that makes it safe to share vulnerable feelings. In fostering any true friendship or personal gift, the crux isn't being a quick study but having the determination to learn by heart.

Contrary to the popular belief that speed is of the essence, what's essential can't be rushed. Speed selling stalls trust. Customer loyalty comes from feeling heard not herded to the register. Consumers can tell the difference between being given a sales job and someone doing a good job in sales. The former is a fast talker. The latter is a slow listener.

In TV ads, the sprint goes to the swift. In life, as in legend, slow and steady wins the race. While a hare-brained scheme can lead to instant short-term success, lasting triumph always entails a long period of persistent plodding. Hares are fleet-footed and can get rich quickly. It takes a tortoise to experience sustained richness. In sum, if you want romance, marry a rabbit. If you want a lasting relationship, go for a turtle. They're not nearly as sexy, but they're steady and they'd rather show up than show off. (And hey, who says endurance isn't endearing?)

Intent

Today I'm content to live in the now and learn at the unhurried pace of a child playing with a pet. (Provided it's a reptile, not a bunny!)

Introspection

Where do you feel pressured to speed up?

Who's a great model of easy-does-it effectiveness?

What can you learn from them that would help you feel less overwhelmed and have a better quality of life?

Implementation

Remember: *What you focus on, you feed.*

At least one time today I will:

This week I will take these two simple steps to lighten my load:
1)

2)

Chapter 9

The Serenity Pause

Inspiration

When it rains, I let it.
~ Response by 113-year-old man explaining the
secret of his longevity.

Photograph by Stephanie Oates

Insight

"It's time!" is a statement that rarely signals a relaxed state of leisure activity. Typically, "It's time," is code for, "Get cracking and get down to business." The stock sentence, "It's time to get serious," is one our job supervisors, external or internal, frequently repeat throughout our workday. "It's time to get serene"? Not so much!

But there's a part in all of us that occasionally just needs to play hooky. A day when we call in well and put up a sign in our own mind that says, "Gone Fishin'."

A slow morning spent picturing ourselves gracefully casting our line, rhythmically reeling it in, and hearing the water lapping against the side of the boat like a liquid melody. Ah, the magic spell of reverie and the calming balm of a brief respite; a time to unwind and a chance to lap it up!

I realize this is a rather fanciful solution. Still, I think it's important to take mental breaks. In light of all the ways we're bombarded at work with demands to get on the stick, there's real value in taking a reprieve from routine and allowing our thoughts to shift from serious to serene. (I'm still working on it!)

My guess is I'm in good company. Odds are, even as you're reading this, your brain's urging you to speed up, not slow down and savor. (Protestant work ethic, forbid!) But what if you didn't have to race through it? Imagine if instead of speed-reading, you were just strolling along line after line, in easy mental rhythm. (Jewish play ethic; try it, you'll like it!)

Here's how it works and how you play. As your eyes take in this next sentence, allow your lungs the luxury of a leisurely, deep breath. Feel your pulse slow and savor your body's built-in capacity to combine deep respiration with relaxed concentration: reading, relaxing, and recharging all in one easy, fluid, simultaneous action. (Now that's my kind of multitasking!)

For all of sixty seconds, shift your heart rate from rapid, shallow, chest breathing to slow, full belly, deep breaths. Hey, if you can't fight or flee, you might as well flow.

As you inhale, picture a place you love. (*Geez*, Rob, now you're asking me to read, relax, and do guided imagery! What next? Transcendental meditation while driving?)

Yeah, I know. Serenity can be a stretch, but it's also a bridge to tranquility that's worth travelling to arrive at. So, go with me on this. Keep reading, breathing, and slowly picturing a place you love: beach, backyard, park bench, beautiful nature trail, waterfall... whatever. Don't overcomplicate it.

As you feel your belly inflate and your chest cavity expand, your mind becomes as clear as a tranquil lake. Without forcing it, you gaze peacefully into the calm waters. Slowly, the lake becomes completely still and you see in its reflection the face of someone you love. (Heck, if you're really serene, you might even see yourself through a very flattering mirror.)

OK, here is the last paragraph linked to one more relaxed, slow, and steady, deep breath. Only this time, as you exhale, expel the air forcefully through your mouth. Trust me, I learned this from a Yoga teacher. He explained the practice of purposefully breathing in through your nose and out through your mouth simultaneously releases more carbon dioxide from the lungs and increases our intake of fresh oxygen to the brain. (Talk about a *twofer!*)

Rest, relax, breathe deeply, and with each heartbeat, feel the flow, and know your soul is on a stroll. No need to fight nor flee. Just take it in, let it go, and you too will live to be 113!

Intent

Today I am calmly breathing in serenity and smoothly breathing out tranquility. Breathing in, I ease my thoughts. Breathing out, I release all tension. Inhaling slowly, I calm my heartbeat. Exhaling serenely, I smile peacefully (and give thanks to Thich Nhat Hanh).

Introspection

Why is it important to you to feel calm and centered?

Where is the place that most consistently eases your mind and allows your body to fully unwind?

Who, besides yourself, would be the main beneficiary of your increased serenity?

Implementation

Remember: *If you write it, you invite it!*

Here's the main thing I'm taking away, and taking action on, today:

My game plan this week is to make these promises to myself come true:
1)

2)

Chapter 10
Relax, Release, Recharge

Inspiration

Sometimes we are smiling because we are happy, and sometimes we are happy because we are smiling.
~ Thich Nhat Hanh, *Peace Is Every Step*

Photograph by Stephanie Oates

Insight

Thich Nhat Hanh is a Vietnamese Buddhist monk with a decidedly Western wit. When asked to conduct a meditation seminar for a group of Type A overachievers in Silicon Valley, his first words were, "Don't just do something, sit there." Whereupon, he warned that if they truly relaxed, they would be "vulnerable to joy."

Then he gently invited them to try a simple, two-sentence, guided visualization meditation. A practice where all they had to do was time their breathing and say to themselves, "Breathing in, I calm my body. Breathing out, I smile." And apparently that was a first for a few of them. Imagine the shock when they found something as simple as smiling could increase their face value!

Thich's simple visualizations and poetic verses such as, "My joy is like spring; so warm, flowers bloom in my hands," have helped my busy brain ease its burdens and experience a quiet serenity. Gradually, I evolved a practice of kindfulness that built on his guided visualization techniques. Here's a short, three-breath sample I welcome you to do right now:

Breathing in, I relax my body.
Breathing out, I release my shoulders.
Breathing in, I picture peaceful mountain lakes.
Breathing out, I feel fear falling away like golden autumn leaves.
Breathing in, I empty my mind and fill my heart with love.
Breathing out slowly, I smile serenely
Voila!

There you have it: a simple, three-breath kindfulness practice applicable for all ages. (Please note: this combination of visualization and meditation has been borrowed from a Buddhist monk, and brought to you by a juggling Jew!)

Intent

Today I am being kindful, taking my time, easing my tension, and finding frequent excuses to smile for no reason.

Introspection

When in your day would doing a simple breathing meditation really come in handy?

How could you use guided imagery as a tool to help you feel less overwhelmed?

Who would be a great person to explore the practice of kindfulness with?

Implementation

Remember: *Specify your steps, magnify your progress.*

To leverage what I learned, my to-do for today is:

Here are two action steps I will accomplish this week:
1)

2)

PART THREE

Being More Self-Aware Brings Better Self-Care

Man who stand on hill with mouth open will wait long time for roast duck to drop in.
~ Confucius

Never Mind My To-Do List, You Should See My Didn't-Do List!

To err is human, but when the eraser wears out ahead of the pencil, you're overdoing it!
~ Josh Jenkins

It's a juggle out there, and it's not easy to get a grip when you've got so many balls in the air you feel like you need to have multiple personalities to handle all your multiple responsibilities! Ah, if only a pharmaceutical giant like Merck could come up with a multiple vitamin that would enhance our capacity to multitask! Smarter and quicker are the magic hooks for ads. You name it, if it purportedly lets us accomplish more in less time, we're as prone to purchase it as we are to pour an additional cup of coffee.

Those three words, "Do more faster," may be the modern credo for efficiency. But when it comes to living a well-balanced life, according to Stephen Covey, who literally wrote the book (and for my music, the bible) on *The Seven Habits of Highly Effective People*, the simple truth is we can't speed up our way to serenity.

The key to developing a high quality of life is to keep an eye on the compass, not on the clock. Conventional time management tools can't lead to better life balance unless they are complemented by a consistent practice of kindfulness.

Combine scheduling downtime into your days without overstressing your nights and you've got a hybrid I call Kind Management. This practice of self-care aligns deeds and creeds in a way that's guided by an inner compass rather than an external clock. The due date is still an important priority. But how we feel as we're doing it becomes a bigger focus. When we practice kindfulness, we remember to build in time for recovery. Bodies aren't built to go full tilt for hours on end. Muscles need rest to recuperate. The same holds true for our brains. Scientific studies conclusively demonstrate that our minds are actually able to concentrate longer and better when we give them periodic breaks.

Kind Management ensures that periods of intense exertion are always counterbalanced by a period of ease that allows both body and brain adequate time to relax and rejuvenate. The happy result is that by regularly recharging our batteries, we can continue to perform at a high level throughout the day, and not drive home at night utterly depleted. In short, Kind Management helps us build in the recovery time we need to keep our working parts in peak order for consistently strong performance.

Chapter 11
Centering & Savoring

Inspiration

Tension is who you think you should be. Relaxation is who you are.

~ Chinese Proverb

Photograph by Wes Page

Insight

Kind Management integrates principles and priorities. One without the other rarely works. We can very efficiently sit at our desks and carefully schedule our calendar. But if we don't build in any time to decompress and recharge, when a door is closed, we're so stressed rather than knock, we barge. (Hint: This is not particularly effective and probably puts a lot of people off!)

By contrast when we practice kindfulness we're less hurried, hence less harried. Both of which makes us less likely to feel hassled, or hung out to dry by other people's unreasonable demands and damn near impossible deadlines. You know you've got good Kind Management skills when it doesn't take much to make you happy and it takes a lot to tick you off!

Ironically, the same social engine that keeps us constantly on overdrive, repeatedly reminds us "time is money!" On the face of it, I'm fine with that idea. Heck, through that lens we can look at downtime as found money! The question is, if being off the clock is so rewarding, why don't we prize leisure and spend less time at our desks?

My hunch is, what chains us is a combination of capitalist competitive drive and socially conditioned Protestant work ethic (seasoned with a generous sprinkling of Jewish thrift!). The consequence is a dangerously intertwined, outward fear of falling behind and internalized pressure to produce. And the more tasks we can accomplish, the more productive we feel (and the less concerned we are that competitors are eating our lunch!).

Being busy becomes a badge of honor. People brag about how full their calendars are, like a packed schedule is a sure sign of success. I've heard several serious Type A overachievers boast that they're so booked, they don't have time to go to the bathroom (which could explain why they're so full of it!). But seriously folks, the problem with living life flat out, pedal to the metal is that keeping our engine in overdrive strains our exhaust system. There's a big difference between feeling driven and being in the driver's seat.

Automotive analogies aside, filling your calendar so you're constantly in demand just becomes too damn demanding! There's no way spending day after day in a flat out sprint leads to a life that's well-rounded. No matter how big your bonus check, when you work at a pace that's the opposite of leisurely, the first casualty is a lack of leisure time.

By contrast, good Kind Management shifts the focus from working faster, harder, and longer to cultivating ways to work smarter and for shorter hours. Instead of feeling driven to acquire material wealth, the goal is to give ourselves, and our loved ones, the priceless gift of free time. Kindfulness doesn't push us to produce ever-increasing external results. Instead, it propels us to reap intrinsic rewards like the peaceful feeling we experience when we're walking in a quiet forest. I know, I know, nobody pays you to take a half-hour walk in the woods. (Ah, but if "time is money," guess what, Honey? You're now thirty minutes richer and three times more relaxed!)

If only serenity was such a cinch. Still, any time invested in slowing the pace, and savoring something calming and centering, is quality time. Being off the clock and in the flow is a surefire way to ease the woe of excess worry. A little time off task to unwind and replenish lets you return to your desk feeling a lot less stressed and a lot more blessed!

At my best, I practice kindfulness by prefacing my workday with something meditative and concluding it with something calming that helps me decompress. I find combining a fifteen-minute, first thing in the morning, breathing meditation with a late afternoon twenty minutes of light stretching to relaxing music, is a Kind Management recipe for sandwiching the daily grind with a pair of mini-vacations. Best of all, this sandwich has zero calories and doesn't add a cent to your work costs. Bottom line: down-time is found money!

But wait, there's more. Bonus free time benefits are yours for the choosing! That's right readers, today, right now (and now only) is the one chance any of us have to be fully in the present. So, why not make it more pleasant by periodically putting on some peaceful music (and for extra credit, close your eyes and treat yourself to a ten-minute, Zen cat-nap where all you do, is be).

Intent

Today I'm making the most of what I've got, by being at peace with who I am, and using kindfulness to find the sweet spot between concentration and relaxation.

Introspection

Why is finding downtime so darn difficult?

When and where are my best opportunities to develop my own practice of kindfulness?

How could a small commitment to better Kind Management have a big impact on my quality of life?

Implementation

Remember: *What you pen on paper, you imprint on your brain.*

Right this minute, I'm marking in a ten-to-fifteen-minute kindfulness slot in my schedule to replenish myself at work by:

Within the week, I will improve my Kind Management by taking time to unwind after each of the following:
1)

2)

3)

Chapter 12

To Task or To Bask

Inspiration

No one can see their reflection in running water. It is only in still water that we can see.

~ Anonymous

Photograph by Jazmine Peck

Insight

If I had to take a wild guess, I'd bet the bulk of just about everyone's job-related stress falls into one big category: overload. You know you're overloaded when your to-do list is a mile long and your didn't-do list stretches into the next zip code.

When we're swamped, technology is often simultaneously the solution and the source of our stress. Computers help us work faster but keep us working longer. There's always one more e-mail to write, post to read, blog link to click, Twitter feed to follow, YouTube video to view, article to download, update to install. Technology can be as much a foe as a friend. (*Eye...Aye...iPad!*)

Hours and hours of staring at a monitor, fingers furiously tapping and clicking, browsing and buying. No wonder our brains are so wired that our bodies find it hard to shut down and get a decent night's sleep. Ah, "...sleep, the innocent sleep, sleep that knits up the raveled sleeve of care..." Alas, instead of deep rest and sweet dreams, we're barraged with disquieting thoughts and nightmares of important items past due. "Macbeth doth murder sleep," and so do missed deadlines.

Like Shakespeare's tortured protagonist, we lament our lost capacity to get a good night's rest, pining for the healing powers of sleep, "...sore labors bath, balm of troubled minds, great nature's second course, chief nurturer in life's feast!"

Bereft of natural replenishment, we revive ourselves by brewing a strong pot of tea or drinking black coffee. In the short run, the caffeine cure works. But while it's possible to raise flowers in a hot house, their bloom is short lived. For sustained growth there's no substitute for the nurturing soil of getting a solid night's sleep on a regular basis. Our bodies and our brains need rest the way fruit trees need water and sunlight to produce a good yield.

However, before you get too tempted to push the pendulum all the way over to long, lazy mornings and afternoon siestas, take heed: too much sleep can lead to sloth! Overdoing anything runs totally counter to Kind Management. Heck, both plants and people relish sunshine. Still, neither benefit from excess exposure. (This despite Mae West's wry credo, "Too much of a good thing is wonderful!")

Striking the right balance of sun and shade, rigor and respite, is the crux of Kind Management. It's finding the sweet spot between discipline and delight. You don't want to be overly diligent, but you also don't want to be so derelict that you become a dilettante! The corollary to the old truism, "All work and no play makes Jack a dull boy," is that all play and no work, makes Jack a jerk.

It's true, we need to tend to tasks, take out the trash, lay down fertilizer, and mulch, but it's also healthy to sit back and bask. For both the garden of our soul, and the vegetables in our backyard, it takes both water and weeding for anything green to grow. But there's no point in harvesting if we don't allow time to enjoy the fruits of our labor. So, here's a toast to planting and feasting, trusting that today's grapes will be tomorrow's wine:

What can we do with our days
but hope and pray
that our dreams bind our work to our play?

What can we do with each moment of our lives,
but love till we've loved it away?
     ~ Bob Franke, Thanksgiving Eve

Intent

Today I'm shifting my mind-set from viewing work and play as a pair of opposites and seeing them instead as synergistic counterparts like the yin and yang.

Introspection

What gets in the way of my making time to play?

Who would be a fun ally to help me co-create more recreational outlets?

When would be the best time to broach this topic with the people who'll be impacted by it the most directly?

Implementation

Remember: *What you articulate, you cultivate.*

Before I close this book, I will write myself a quick reminder that:

By the end of this week there will be a pair of checkmarks next to these two to-do's:

1)

2)

Chapter 13

Corral Chaos, Court Order

Inspiration

Mindfulness helps us separate the grain from the chaff, pare away the husks, sift what is worth keeping, and gently blow away the rest.

~ Paraphrase of Jon Kabat Zinn and Kahlil Gibran

Photograph by Stephanie Oates

Insight

Eastern cultures have perfected an art of using indoor greenery to replicate the beauty of the outdoors. This craft allows them to create a more peaceful work, or home environment, through a quality of orderly placement called Feng Shui.

As with plants, so too with paperwork. There is a time to preserve and a time to prune. Piles need to be pared into files, bills paid, birthday cards sent, and new children's drawings displayed. (Prior sentimental favorites delegated to the one who prizes them most for safekeeping, the rest ruthlessly relegated to the recycling bin.)

God grant me decisiveness and discretion "...and the wisdom to know the difference."

"Aye, there's the rub!" (The Serenity Prayer and Shakespeare, what a pair!) To paraphrase Hamlet's timeless soliloquy:

> *To keep, or not to keep? That is the question. Whether 'tis nobler in the mind to suffer the dings and pop-ups of outrageous overload, or by opposing, filter them.*

Parody aside, dramatizing the need to de-clutter and dispose is a classic case of teaching what I most need to learn. I'm so far from mastering the quality of simplicity and spaciousness of Feng Shui, I must have been the poster child for Feng *Shwamped*! As a habitual hoarder and sentimental fool, who's far better at treasuring than tossing, I cringe when efficiency experts promote scrapping over saving (mercilessly pointing out that the more you purge, the less you pile).

I yearn to practice the approach those who are most proficient at paperwork call OHIO (only handle it once). The goal is to take immediate action. Deal with it and be done with it. Open the envelope, quickly scan the contents, and either toss it or take care of it, right there and then. Either way, you'll never have it in your hand again.

By sad contrast, my model is more mull it over, put it aside, procrastinate, and add it to the pending pile, creating an ever-burgeoning stack that I blissfully rationalize I'll someday file. On the plus side, if procrastinating ever has the same effect on paperwork that marinating has on meat, I'll have me a gourmet desk! Oh, how I wish. For the moment, what I've got is more like a three-dimensional, totally disheveled, patchwork quilt of backdated periodicals, photos in need of frames, unfinished books, unsorted mail, unfiled program notes, and UPOs (unidentifiable piling objects).

Oh well. The good side of Kind Management is that rather than beat myself up for my shortcomings, I bless my flaws for teaching me to take myself lightly. I have faith that as long as I don't run myself down, in time I'll come up with a work-around. Bottom line: The core of Kind Management is the compassionate self-talk that patiently says, "Hang in there." As opposed to my inner critic (I've named him Boris Taskt) who glowers at me disdainfully and shouts, "Hang it up!"

So, for now, I tip my hat to those admirably efficient types who proficiently manage paperwork by practicing OHIO, with truly paperless offices because they only handle it once, whereas my state is more like MISSISSIPPI (maybe I should save it since someday it'll possibly prove important).

Intent

Today I'm cheerfully turning over a new leaf and pruning my piles into ploughshares, singing "Down by the Riverside"!

Introspection

Why do I wind up holding on to stuff for too long?

Where would letting go get me going down a better path?

How can I use Kind Management to counter-balance my inner critic?

Implementation

Remember: *What you write down, you invite in!*

OK, enough is enough. Today's the day I:

This week I will carve out time for the following Kind Management action steps:
1)

2)

3)

Chapter 14

Rob's Recipe for Renewal

Inspiration

*I arise in the morning torn between a desire to improve the world
and a desire to enjoy the world.
This makes it hard to plan the day!*
~ E.B. White

Photograph by Stephanie Oates

Insight

At any age, preventive medicine plays a pivotal role in maintaining a positive mental outlook. For me, consistent Kind Management requires a steady adherence to healthy regimens of sleep, hygiene, diet, exercise, vitamins, and medicines. A key corollary to pragmatic routine is creating rituals of renewal; daily kindfulness practices that nurture my spiritual, emotional, and mental fitness. That's the good news.

The bad news is between professional demands, parental duties, and periodic fires I have to put out on the spot, self-managing my regimens is a constant challenge.

Like E.B. White, I arise torn. For me, the question is, "How to get off on the right foot, in a left-brain world?" Alas, I'm not any clearer come bedtime. How to get to sleep serenely when my schedule's still crammed with a long list of to-do's, didn't-do's, and really-need-to-get-to's!

Fortunately, I've found the way I start my day when I first arise, is a time period reliably under my control. Slowly but successfully, I've created daily rituals of renewal. In hopes it will prove good grist for the mill, I've listed the ingredients below.

Rob's Recipe for Waking up on the Bright Side of the Bed

Step One: Take two minutes to lie in bed and greet the morning with three reasons to feel grateful (including the absence of past ailments or easing of present ones).

Step Two: Sit up and savor the simple pleasure of several slow, relaxing, deep breaths. (For extra credit, as you inhale, picture faces of people precious to you. Imagine, as you exhale, all aches and fears falling away like golden autumn leaves lilting softly to earth.)

Step Three: Lie on your back in bed and spend five to seven minutes slowly stretching opposite limbs, shaping your body in the shape of an extended X. (Take care to notice where you're tight and see if you can discover a gentle way to move that eases the tension.)

Step Four: Be mindful of your jaw responding to muscle tightness by clenching, and counter this reaction by lightly opening your lips and placing your tongue at the bottom of your mouth. (Better yet, fix your face in a broad smile that signals relaxation to your brain.)

Step Five: Roll out of bed, open the blinds, and weather permitting, lift the window. Stick your head out and smell the morning. Take a firm stance, raise both arms over your head triumphantly, and say, "Yes!" (And if that's too over the top, just a little, quick wink at your own reflection in the mirror will suffice.)

Step Six: When it's warm out, brush your teeth in the sun and feel lucky that this lets you spend a few extra minutes outdoors on a nice day. (And for extra oral hygiene, be sure you start by vigorously brushing your tongue. My dentist's tip that this scrapes off bacteria that build up over the night has greatly decreased my susceptibility to sinusitis, sore throats, and head colds.)

Step Seven: Pour a tall glass of water or fruit juice, and before fixing breakfast, sit in a quiet spot. As you slowly drain the liquid, jot down the names of three people your gut tells you would welcome a small gesture of kindness. As you down the last swallow, raise the glass in a toast to starting your day with kindfulness practices that fill you with a spirit of gratitude and generosity.

Bonus Step: On those rare, tip-top mornings when you really do roll out of bed feeling fully alive, spend another twenty to thirty seconds by the window belting out an upbeat tune that befits the outdoor conditions: "Grey Skies Are Going to Clear Up," "Good Day Sunshine," "I'm Singing in the Rain," "On the Sunny Side of the Street," "Let It Snow! Let It Snow! Let It Snow!"

Intent

Today I am smilingly reminding myself that taking good care of my body is making great use of my brain!

Introspection

Remember: *What you spell out sends in a signal to your will.*

What impedes my chances of creating Kind Management rituals of renewal?

Who's the most in-my-corner person who would be my best resource to reach out to for support?

When, and where, would create the ideal circumstances for you to kick-start a collaborative brainstorm on better self-care?

Implementation

Before I read another page, I will jot myself a note to ensure that I follow through on:

My focus this month is to budget into my weekly schedule these two specific activities to deepen my capacity for Kind Management:
1)

2)

PART FOUR

Artistic Alternatives

A Sneak Peak at Peck's
Creative Streak in
Poetry & Prose

Chapter 15

Photograph by Jeff Boudro

A Poet's Alternative to a Personal Ad

SWM who believes there are some questions that can't be answered (but no answers that can't be questioned!) seeks a relationship that evolves like Glendale Falls. It begins as a small, slow moving brook. There is nothing forced. Everything occurs in a relaxed, natural progression. The current is unseen, the surface waters gently streaming like Jimmy

Buffet strumming a six-string guitar. The rhythm has a liq-
uid-like quality of going with the flow, effortlessly picking
the path of least resistance. Its trajectory isn't flat, but it
doesn't dip or arch steeply. The pheromones are bubbling
but not bursting with such force they flood the banks. Time
is unnoticeable and delightfully inconsequential. Nature is
off the clock. The brook's softly splashing percussion provides a steady backbeat as soothingly pleasant as a baby's
merry babbling.

Glendale Falls never bogs down in conformity. It's the
living antithesis of same old, same old monotony. It's a relationship between river and rocks that thrives on variety and
unpredictability.

There is a moment, a tender look, when eyes smile in
tandem. Then there is a quickening of the pulse, a rise in the
current, and an almost imperceptible narrowing of the
banks. Boundaries aren't blurred, but borders become less
about separating and more about guiding further progress.
The brook expands into a stream.

A little dip around a bend, leaning a little closer into
one another, dancing, and a small vortex starts to swirl. The
pace of the stream accelerates around a cluster of rocks and
the current kicks into a higher gear. The tops of underwater
boulders rise up like sentries, bras blocking taut nipples. But
now the momentum is too strong. It can't be checked, and in
a giddy triumph of connectivity, the liquid and the solids
commune. Breasts are bared, and the stream becomes a river.

There is a playful pushing and pulsing, as the river
and the rocks feed off of each other's yin and yang. One is
hard and offers solidity and stability. The other is soft and

supple, and slides easily over, around, and through the other's tight places.

Suddenly the terrain shifts dramatically. The river slants downward at a rakish angle. Discovering the pathways between the rocks becomes a more challenging task. Both sides raise their game, and the churning currents froth with sparkling vitality.

The rocks deftly diversify their shapes and formations. The river adroitly responds with an equally versatile repertoire. Sometimes oozing over smooth, mossy stones and spilling over flat surfaces in ways that cause the rocks to glisten in the sun like cut glass. Other times, the rippling waters tumble down a stone stairwell, splashing loudly as laughing, first-grade school kids rolling down a steeply sloping lawn, into a thick pile of autumn leaves. And still, other times the river transubstantiates into a kind of liquid drill sluicing a channel between sheer ledge.

This is lovemaking that's never twice the same. A jubilant defiance to all those who insist there's nothing new under the sun. It is harmony in motion and a ringing affirmation of nature's limitless creativity.

At some point downstream, its angles become less steep, but the falls are never sterile. Even where its trajectory levels off, the river is still teeming with life. Here little pools coalesce and cool refreshments beckon. There is a sense of replenishment and a quiet gathering of strength. These are the conversational lulls when words give way to gazes and gentle caresses; palms gently lapping over legs and hindquarters, softly stroking and brushing smooth skin and silky hair. These pooling waters are the pillow talk that is prologue to passion.

The ripples swirling at their outer edges belie the centers' seeming stillness. They silently signal a powerful undercurrent. Our conversation may slow, but our connection is never stagnant. Our bodies' rhythms, like the river's transpositions, constantly transform themselves. Tumbling and turning, the waterfalls envelope our senses in an enchanted moving tapestry; a liquid landscape, endlessly providing confluent sights and sounds, and striking new discoveries.

The relationship I seek is as constantly renewing as the interplay of river and rocks; a connection whose vision is rewarded in all directions. For just as the river and the rocks conjoin in yin-yang harmony, there is a symmetrical blending of upstream and downstream, of storytelling and shared listening. A musical fountain, made ever more melodious by the happy juxtaposition of cascading waters and glimmering sunbeams gracefully giving way to moonshine. Breadths of rippling light fanning out in all directions; a delicious balancing act and perfect vantage point to soak in every moist note. A place of peace, like a Zen bridge, that lets us look on either side to see where the symphony was, and where the symphony is going.

If this sounds good to you, please inquire within!

Chapter 16

Photograph by Jeannette Tokarz

The Flowers O' Friendship

Some friends are like wildflowers. The relationships seem to bloom of themselves like favorite cousins at a family celebration, annual conference buddies, high school teammates, or old college pals. All it takes is proximity, and presto! The colors of these friendships burst forth in exuberant profusion. The minute we lay eyes on these kinds of flowers their radiance is instantly available and immediately gratifying. Like time-lapse photography, all the months apart magically compress and we pick up where we left off as easily as picking daisies for a fresh bouquet.

As reliably as rain waters garden beds, our attention is rooted in the here and now, mutually savoring and warmly appreciating each other's new leaves, buds, and hues. The air is charged with an intensely energizing fragrance. Our senses are suffused with beauty, interconnectedness, and abundance. Best of all, this emotional cornucopia requires no preparation and almost zero maintenance. Rain, sun, and soil feed and nurture these wildflowers so naturally their upkeep requires very little attention and effort.

Other friendships are like garden flowers. They are not quite so self-sufficient. For these friendships to succeed we have to weed and mulch a little. But the results of our TLC are well worth it. A quick card, short phone call, or fast "Saw this and thought of you," e-mail quickly resuscitates these flowers' vibrancy. The spontaneous invitation to enjoy their company for a leisurely stroll is a reliable source of comfort. Conversations circle around to mutual concerns, fostering the deep sharing that provides fertile soil for meaningful reflection. These garden flower friendships brighten our view, lighten our step, and help us get outdoors more often.

Our inner circles of friends are more like houseplants. These can't simply be left to Mother Nature to nurture. They require regular watering with check-in phone calls, stop by visits, short walks, heart-to-heart talks, shared meals, and above all, reciprocal support. These plants sometimes droop and wither. They also snap back and sprout new growth that gladdens everything around them.

These are our indoor friends, the ones we don't just run into on the street, at concerts, or conferences. The ones we welcome into our homes and around our hearths. Their roots stretch into the deepest soil of our souls and become so entwined with our own, the laughter and tears that wash over one waters the other. These friendships weather winter together and are seasoned by many springs. Lasting relationships grow like conifers in summer. Their branches don't turn bare in autumn. Their time-tested character stays ever-green, their boughs both faithful and forgiving. These are the friends whose photosynthesis we can count on to take the carbon monoxide of our distress and turn it into the oxygen of our connectedness.

There is both art and science to friendship. Beyond the art and the science, there is also the spiritual wonder, which when years turn to decades, transforms a select few houseplants into bonsai trees. And these graced friendships are never left behind when we move. They remain rooted in our hearts for the rest of our lifetime. Wildflowers, garden flowers, and houseplants all add a vital luster to our days. But it is the bonsai trees that get us through the long nights, bind our wounds, and are our most enduring source of true wealth.

Chapter 17

Photograph by Jim Adgate

Song for Spring's Golden Gate

When spring has sprung in San Francisco,
It's like a farmer let a field lay fallow.
The trees are hung low with blossoms like snow,
The old feel young, even the sallow glow.
Because spring has sprung in San Francisco!

Buskers on Pier 39 put on a mighty fine show,
With each sleight of hand fake, they slyly rake in the dough.
They know to earn their keep,
They've got to reap what they sow,

'Cause that's the law of the street in San Francisco.

When spring has sprung in San Francisco,
It's like a farmer let a field lay fallow.
The trees are hung low with blossoms like snow,
The old feel young, even the sallow glow.
Because spring has sprung in San Francisco!

Cable cars clang like Bennett sang long ago,
When Tony left part of his heart in San Francisco.
Trolley lines climb streets steep and narrow,
At the crest gazing west, you see the sun sink low,
Each ray bathing the bay with a Golden Gate glow.

Well, the tide can't hide what the sage ones know.
When the city sparkles like a halo,
And all of Nature is in free flow,
Winter's done and on the run in Frisco.

When spring has sprung in San Francisco,
It's like a farmer let a field lay fallow.
The trees are hung low with blossoms like snow,
The old feel young, even the sallow glow.
Because spring has sprung in San Francisco!

The season is the reason that this song has been sung.
Now you know the time has come,
And spring has sprung
In San Francisco.

Chapter 18

Photograph by Jeff Boudro

Pizza Hanukkah

It was in my pocket all day. I'd forgotten about it until the little Hungarian boy asked, "Isn't Hanukkah where you play dreidel?" My fingers knew just where to go, and the look on his face when he saw it appear in my palm was the best present anyone's given me in a long time.

As his fingers reached out excitedly to hold it, my mind flashed over the circuitous route that had brought us to this moment. My thirteen-year-old daughter, Jazmine, and I had begun the day at my dad's house in Tenafly, New Jersey. Jazz and Grandpop teamed up on a fun pancake breakfast. Then I packed the car for a day in the Big Apple, before heading home to New England. As we were loading our luggage, my father walked across the driveway and pushed the small, beveled wooden dreidel into my hand, insisting, "Take it with you. I'm too old for this." I was so intent on getting our suitcases in the trunk I said, "Ok, thanks," and pocketed it.

After waving Grandpop farewell, Jazz and I drove off, parked the car in Fort Lee, and took public transport into the city to meet my boyhood pal, Charles, at his office in Bloomingdale's department store. The plan was that, in lieu of him giving me a Hanukkah gift, Charles would use his store discount to treat my daughter to a piece of posh apparel. Jazz considered this a great present, and the two of them hit it off famously.

Jazz picked out a chic skirt and embroidered shirt. She was also the beneficiary of numerous Bloomie, freebie perfume bracelets. With each new item, her eyes lit up, warming me and my buddy in their glow. By the end of the shopping spree, Charles' own face was shining with such vicarious glee, I could almost see my boyhood friend grow younger.

Beaming like a trio of school kids who'd just gotten an extra period on the playground, we exited the store and headed to the subway. After giving us careful instructions on switching trains, and making sure to catch the uptown express, Charles quickly embraced me goodbye then turned to face Jazz. Her face gleaming with appreciation, she opened her arms wide, and thanked her benefactor with a bear hug.

We reached 175th Street, exited, and grabbed the first bus going across the George Washington Bridge. We got off in Fort Lee, walked a few short blocks, hopped in my trusty Toyota Echo, and headed back to sweet New England. Thankfully, there was little traffic, and the ride was made even smoother listening to Jim Dale's inspired, audio rendition of J.K Rowling's *Harry Potter and the Prisoner of Azkaban*. By the second CD, the skies were dark. Halfway through the third disc, Jazz's head began to droop. Summoning her last bit of consciousness, she nestled her head sideways against the headrest, smiled beatifically, and managed two last words before conking out, "Dinner... pizza."

"Sounds good, Pal. You rest now. I'll wake you up when it's time to eat."

It had been time for dinner a good hour already, and alas, I hadn't seen any sign for pizza. Fortunately, my kiddo's fatigue still had the upper hand on her hunger, and she dozed peacefully beside me. I peered intently at each highway placard's offerings: McDonalds, Friendly's, Dunkin' Donuts, Burger King, Roy Rogers. Exit after exit, every roadside eatery imaginable, and not a single pizza joint in the bunch.

Another long hour went by and still no luck. By now, my stomach was voicing its own opinion. Its loud growling probably woke Jazz up.

"Hi, Dad. Where are we?" Jazz yawned.

"We're in Connecticut," I replied.

"I'm hungry, can we eat dinner soon?" she asked plaintively.

"Pal, your papa's been trying and trying to find you pizza. But all I've seen are signs listing every other fast food place you can think of."

"Dad, can we stop soon? I'm starvin'!"

"I hear ya, Pal. Tell you what, I'll pull into the next place that's open and see if maybe somebody knows of a pizzeria that's off the highway, but not too far away."

"OK. Thanks, Dad," she replied, sounding reassured.

At the next exit, I pulled into an Exxon station to ask about somewhere to buy pizza. The guy pumping gas next to me said he was pretty sure a small, new pizza place called Papa John's stayed open till 9:00 p.m. I checked my watch and saw it was already 8:45 p.m. The guy told me the place is less than ten minutes away. I figured it was our best hope, quickly got directions, and jumped back into my car.

My haste made me waste a precious minute turning around and retracing my route back to where I was supposed to turn. I checked the time, and realized one more wrong turn and we were screwed. I gripped the wheel like I was driving a race car. Just as we arrived at the correct intersection, I saw coming towards me, like a vision in the night, a car with a big, lit up sign on the roof illuminating three words, one in all caps: PIZZA.

I tapped Jazz's knee and pointed. The beacon drew nearer. When I could make out the other two words, *We Deliver*, I was ready to believe it was a sign from G-d! The vehicle, with two slightly long-haired, middle-aged men in it, slowly crossed the intersection. I honked twice and the driver stopped across from us.

We simultaneously rolled down our windows and I said, "Thanks for stopping."

He answered smilingly, "No problem. Are you lost?"

"No," I replied, "Just hungry. Can you deliver to a car?"

"I don't know. Nobody ever asked me that before. My shop's just a few miles up the road. Why don't you follow me, and we'll see if there's still some slices left. You with me?"

"Right behind you, and I sure hope you do, 'cause I've got a kiddo here who's had a hankering for pizza since 6:00 p.m." Jazz nodded vigorously in agreement.

He added, encouragingly, "Alright, tell you what. Normally, we close at nine o'clock. But it's my shop, so worse comes to worst, I'll put one last pie in the oven. Sound good?"

"Sounds great!" I exclaimed. "Thank you. You're the answer to our prayers!"

For the first time, the other passenger piped up, saying in a thick, Balkan accent, "Is good. You follow. We make hot. No go hungry."

He punctuated his pidgin English with a big grin; a smile that was somehow warmly reassuring despite revealing several missing teeth. I flashed a thumbs-up signal, and as if on cue, we closed our windows with the same synchronized precision that we opened them. After three or four miles, I saw a sign for Papa John's. We parked beside the delivery car and followed our two saviors inside. The second we entered, several small children scooted behind the front counter. The place was tiny and clearly designed for takeout orders, with only a big counter, one small table, and a couple chairs. A woman in an apron stood in front of a large oven.

Another one came out of a side room, and immediately the three little girls and one slightly older boy raced over to her.

The man who owned the shop explained that we were there after hours by his invitation and asked the woman with the apron if there were any slices left. She shook her head "No." The other man, with the gap-toothed smile quickly turned to us and said, "No worry. You eat. We make pie."

Nodding, the shop owner extended his hand and said, "I'm John. You just tell me what size pie you want and I'll have it ready for you in ten minutes. Large, medium, small, whatever you want."

My belly instantly voted for large. My mind leaned more toward medium. But my frugality made a unilateral decision to order a small.

John smiled, "OK, small it is. Give me ten minutes, and it'll be ready."

In the three seconds it took to nod my assent and say thanks, a crazy notion showed up full-born in my brain. It was the sixth night of Hanukkah, and each of the preceding nights Jazz had been pumped to observe the traditional rituals of candle lighting and jointly singing the Hebrew song of holiday blessing. Even though it had gotten late, I didn't want her to miss out on one of the last three nights of celebration.

My brainwave was, "We've got ten minutes to kill anyway, why not go back to the car and get out the menorah from the trunk?" We could set it up on the glove compartment, and once the candles were lit, Jazz could open the little present I'd surreptitiously purchased at Bloomingdale's Gourmet section for the occasion.

Happily, the minute I gave voice to what I was think-ing, Jazz was completely onboard. As we headed out to the car, two of the little kids peeked around the counter to watch us. *Shazzam!* My wild idea took a turn for the crazier. Maybe instead of doing our ritual out in the car all by ourselves, we should bring the menorah inside, and invite the kids to gather around it.

When I tried to put it into words, my thoughts sud-denly shifted from how to involve the kids, to whether my teenager would think the idea was so weird it would finally force her to enter me into the Fathers Who Embarrass Their Daughters in Public Hall of Fame! Bracing myself for the in-evitable, "No way, Dad! What're you, nuts?"

I gingerly broach the subject. "Hey Pal, did you notice those little kids when we first came in?"

"Yeah, they were cute the way they hid," she replied.

"Weren't they? And you know what? I'll bet they never saw a Hanukkah menorah in their life."

"Duh!" She rolled her eyes.

I continued, cautiously. "Well, I'm just thinking aloud here. But I have a hunch lighting the candles and all would really fascinate them,"

Jazz turned her face quickly and shot me the teen daughter look with deadly accuracy. I recognized it instant-ly. Of course, I'd had ample past experience with *the look*: a freeze-you-in-your-tracks combination of incredulity, laced with irritation.

"Da-*ahd*, it's a restaurant! Their customers come there to order food, not to celebrate religious holidays. *Hello?*"

I realized she was never going to go for it and tried to hide a small sigh of resignation. I wasn't going to say anything more about it, when that stubborn part of reptilian dad-brain got a surge of willpower.

"You're right, Pal. It's a totally wacky notion. And yet, maybe because Christmas was only a couple days ago, they'd be open to making an exception. Who knows? They might even be a little curious about what happens for Hanukkah, and kind of glad for their children to see such a fun part of the holiday."

Jazz shrugged. "OK, Dad. If they say it's alright, I'm fine with doing the candles inside. But I'm not going to be the one to try to get permission for such a weird request. If you want to do Hanukkah in a takeout pizza place, you gotta be the one who's crazy enough to ask for it."

"Fair enough," I said, "I'll ask, and if — and I realize it's a big *if* — they say it's OK, I really appreciate your willingness to try something so out of the ordinary."

Jazz shot me an impish smile and replied, "You're the one who's taking the risk, Pop. I'm not asking such a strange favor, you are."

"True enough. I know they might think it's too weird. But what the hell, we'll never know if we don't ask, right?"

"Yup," she confirmed.

"I love you, Angel," I replied.

"I love you, too, and I hope for your sake they say yes." She smiled benevolently.

"Thanks, Pal. But I think, just to up the odds, I'll bring in the menorah and box of candles, so at least they'll get a better idea of why I think it might be so fun for their kids."

As we walk back in, my mind races to line up the right words. But the minute John looks up at me, I abandon all hope of diplomacy, and blurt out, "Hey, I know this is a bizarre request. But even though Christmas is over, Hanuk-kah's still going on, and well, I was wondering if it might be an interesting thing for your kids to see how Jewish people celebrate by lighting this menorah?"

Sure enough, the image of his kids seeing colored candles all aglow in a vintage, brass candelabra piqued John's curiosity. With a bemused expression, he leaned over the counter and scratched his head.

"I don't know. Nobody's ever asked me that before."

His sidekick flashed another broad smile and said, "Yes, do. Is good kids see."

Thankfully, the children didn't need a second invita-tion. The moment I placed the menorah down on the tiny table, they circled around like it was a campfire. The light in their eyes was so bright, Jazz's teen coolness melted. In no time, the circle of eager faces kindled her own childlike en-thusiasm.

Eyes sparkling, Jazz began demonstrating how we light the center candle, called the Shamos, so its flame can soften the bottom wax of the others to ensure they'll stay up-right. In short order, the sight and smell of the burning wax created a ritual effect of sacred space. One by one, Jazz gracefully invited each little child to take a turn and gently assisted them in igniting the wicks without burning their fingers. When there were still two extra candles to go, she looked up at one of the women hovering just outside the cir-cle and wordlessly welcomed her to do the honors. Shyly, she accepted, and in turn, beckoned her friend to do the final candle.

Between the fullness of the flames and the increase in our circle, my wild idea grew wilder. As if it's the most natural thing in the world, I began to recount the story behind the ritual of lighting the candles. Midway through describing the role of the Maccabees, I snuck a peak at Jazz. Her eyes beamed back at me as brightly as the glowing wicks. I could tell she was with me all the way. I paused in my narrative, hoping she would pick up on my cue, and joined in the telling. Jazz chimed right in with such compelling enthusiasm both the kiddos and the women leaned closer.

Our dad-daughter, tandem telling took on such a smoothly spontaneous rhythm of passing the baton and picking up on where the other left off, I didn't want the story to ever end. Yet, when I reached the climactic discovery of the one small jar of oil, it was clear that Jazz needed to be the one to reveal the miracle that makes the tale so inspiring. She pulled it off with such verve, the kids literally jumped for joy.

The oldest — a thin, wiry, boy with dark, tousled hair and deep seated brown eyes — looked up at Jazz and said, "I can't believe it. That one little jar of oil burned eight times longer than it ever had before. That's amazing!"

Her own intensity rising proportionately, Jazz replied, "You got it! That little jar was so miraculous it's become a Jewish tradition to remember it every year at this time, with eight candles, one for each night the oil stayed lit."

At this point, I was so into it, I blurted out to John, "If you want to hear it, there's also a traditional song of rejoicing we sing. It might be a little weird cause it's in Hebrew." Suddenly, mindful of the look, I paused in midsentence, gazing furtively at my daughter. Jazz didn't say a word, but to my happy relief, the only thing I saw in her eyes was an unequivocal, green light. I broke into a smile that soon became a silly grin when John said, "I don't know. Nobody's ever asked me that before!"

The onlookers implored us to sing. Jazz nodded affirmatively and started us off on just the right note. My singing (always spotty at best) soon veered off-key. But Jazz's vocals were so clear, strong, and persuasive she steered me back, and midway we performed a sort of minor, modern-day Hanukkah miracle, finishing in harmony.

When we stopped, everybody clapped. Then one of the littlest said with poignant candor, "What happens next? Is that the end? Isn't there anymore?"

I was temporarily stymied. Fortunately, Jazz's better angels rose and she responded, "No way! Now comes the best part, presents!" Suddenly realizing the expectation she raised, Jazz reached into her pocket and warmly placed the Bloomie's perfume bracelet around the little girl's wrist.

The young recipient's face lit up with grateful surprise. The look, like the candle lighting, passed onto adjacent faces as each child in turn reacted with similar glee to receiving their own unexpected gifts. Even the boy seemed delighted to strap on his Bloomie bracelet. Then Jazz turned and looked at me expectantly. I hastily excused myself, dashed back to the car, and quickly return with the fancy chocolate bar I knew was her all-time favorite.

The second she spotted it, Jazz's teen sophistication vanished, and she tore off the wrapper like a five-year-old opening her shiniest birthday present.

"Daddy, you got me the Gold Bullion Bar! I love it. Thank you so much. You're the best!"

To my paternal joy, she started breaking off squares for each of the children and even offered some to their mothers.

By then, the ritual energy was so magnetic both men were drawn into the circle. I didn't want the magic to end but couldn't think of anything else to do.

Presto! That's when the boy piped up, "Isn't Hanukkah where you play dreidel?"

As I took it out of my pocket, my mind flashed on my father's favorite saying about serendipity: "Life sometimes works out better than anyone could plan!" Little did I know that the unplanned still had a few more wrinkles.

The young boy tried several times in vain to get the dreidel to spin. Then his uncle, Ray, the man with the gap-toothed smile, came to his rescue. "I used to play this toy. We call tops when I was boy in Hungary. Give here. I try make for you good spin."

With great concentration, he coiled the dreidel in his fingers, snapped his wrist, and shot the toy right off the table. The children burst into laughter. But all of them combined were no match for the Hungarian's huge belly laugh at himself. Retrieving the dreidel, he handed it to me and said, still quaking with laughter, "Here, you better teacher."

I winked playfully at him, deliberately mimed his intense concentration, and managed to make the dreidel careen even more akimbo. Jazz's gleeful chortle rivaled the Hungarian's. Buoyed by his elder's incompetence, the little boy tried again, and to everyone's delight succeeded in not only keeping it on the table, but briefly getting it to spin.

"And lo, a little child shall lead them," I reflected.

Grinning almost maniacally, the Hungarian motioned for the dreidel, saying, "OK, you my teacher, give here. I learn you example." Sure enough, some of his old form returned and the dreidel had a good long spin. I followed suit with a similarly long spin, and likewise credited the boy for my success.

Emboldened by his two elders acknowledging him as their teacher, the lad reclaimed the dreidel, and for the next several minutes we all cheered him on as his skill steadily improved. Jazz and I got so caught up in his growing excitement, we plumb forgot all about our pizza until a bell dinged in the back of the restaurant. A moment later, John returned with the pie in a flat take-out box.

"One minute," I said, "I've got a ten in my wallet."

"No need," he responded, with a gleam in his eye. "The pizza's your present." His brother Ray vigorously nodded in assent.

My first reaction was to protest. "Wait, that's so nice of you. But that's not part of the deal here. You've all made us so welcome tonight. That's present enough."

John looked at me, and somehow found a way to simultaneously smile broadly and say, "No!"

Nonplussed, I sought to at least negotiate a compromise. "Listen. This is so generous of you, it's too much. Please, trust me. I'd feel a lot better if you'd at least let me pay you half, and believe me, the other half would still be a great gift."

John fixed me in his gaze, and again his smile widened even as he firmly shook his head no. "It's Hanukkah right? And you and your daughter made my whole family happy the way you shared this wonderful holiday here with us. So, please, this is my way of saying, thank you!"

Finally, I got it. Much as I never intended it, and in fact wanted him to receive payment to help his new business, John's sense of having received a present from us and wanting to give one back was so pure, anything less than a full acceptance would affront his integrity. Luckily, my lips needn't be nearly as nimble to manage to both smile and say, "Thank you."

Jazz and I were genuinely touched, and for a moment, the two chatterbox Jews were speechless. Each of us just looked around with a happy, idiot grin on our faces. Then I noticed the Menorah was almost extinguished and said, "Before we go, I wonder if any of you would like to make a wish and blow out the candles?"

True to form, John shot me a pensive look, and said with a Cheshire cat grin, "I don't know. Nobody ever asked me that before!"

We weren't through chuckling when, to my surprise, the oldest boy quickly stepped forward and bowed his head. After a brief silence, he startled me still further by reciting his wish aloud. "I hope every year at Christmastime we can also celebrate Hanukkah and play dreidel."

As he solemnly raised his head, I caught Jazz's eye and sensed her complicity. For the third time that day my fingers closed around the little dreidel in my pocket. Wordlessly, I removed it, nodded to Jazz, who flashed me a million dollar smile, and offered it to the boy. Reverently, he took it from my palm, looked gratefully from me to Jazz, and said, "Thank you both, I will never forget this. I promise."

Jazz beat me to it and gave him a big hug. I put my arms around the two of them and said, "You're very welcome."

I notice his mom wipe away a tear, and next thing I knew she was hugging all three of us. Soon, everybody crowded around, and I got hugged by everyone, including John, who was laughing; and his brother Ray, who was crying.

Finally, Jazz got all the kids to join her in blowing out the candles, and as we left, the littlest girl plaintively asked her dad, "Can we do Hanukkah again next year at Christmas?"

"I don't know," John responds, stroking his chin thoughtfully. Then before he can say it, his son gleefully shouts, "Nobody's ever asked him that before!"

We were still laughing as we made ready to leave. Two steps from the door, Ray stopped us, and said in his thick, Hungarian accent, "What people say in war *not* true! Many soldiers bad to Jews. Is sad. After war some come live in village. They good to me. I learn Jews smart people and have big hearts. I glad you eat our food."

I couldn't think of how to respond. John rescued me and chimed in, "My older brother knows a lot more about Jews than I do. I was too young to fight. We just came to the States two years ago, and all our friends are Hungarian. So far, I haven't gotten to know any Jewish people. But if they're all as kind as you and your daughter, I know I'm missing something. I hope you enjoy your pizza and you visit us again."

"Thank you", Jazz quickly replied. "You and your family are so nice and so generous, I'm sure we will." To which I could only add, "John, if I'd known you people would feel this good about Jews, never mind the small, I'd have ordered a large!"

The pie was still hot in my hands as we waved good-bye and walked out to the sight of the little boy waving the dreidel, the owner slapping his knee, and the sound of the Hungarian's howling laughter billowing like joyful thunder.

PART FIVE

Reader's Reward
Bonus Transcript of One-Hour
Webinar on Life Balance:
Keeping All the Balls in the
Air... *Not!*

7 Simple Steps to Reduce Overload & Feel Less Overwhelmed

This section is the complete text of a stress management webinar I created for The Association for Part-time Professionals (TAPP). Relevant slides have been described briefly, and while I've made a few modifications to help with the absence of the slides, this is the essence of the TAPP webinar to help reduce the stress of overload and overwhelm.

Welcome to today's webinar. My name is Rob Peck, and I'll be your tour guide as we explore the six steps of laughing, learning, and part-time earning a living doing what you love. There will now be a slight pause while many of you scratch your heads and wonder, "Who the heck is Rob Peck?"

(Slide: Famous namesakes.)

Check it out, Academy Award Winner, Gregory Peck; prizewinning author, M. Scott Peck (clearly I'm from a distinguished lineage... I wish!). Well, as you can probably tell, ordinarily I like to take myself lightly. But right now, my sinuses are so heavily congested, I'm afraid for the next sixty minutes my voice is going to be (pretty much) a bad blend of Bruno Kirby and Joe Pesci with a head cold!

But enough about me. From what little I know about you, looks like we've got a wide range of folks from very different circumstances who share common challenges. Many, me included, are working for themselves from home and to make ends meet, occasionally have to moonlight. (In my case, as a part-time, nonprofit, fundraising consultant and live auctioneer.)

(Slide: Me in a formal tux at a recent event.)

Aside from being such a snappy dresser at celebratory auctions, my three chief qualifications for giving this webinar are:

1. I've raised a child who's now graduated college.
2. I developed and direct my own company, Zestworks Speaking & Training.
3. Neither of the first two reasons has sent me to the poor house, yet!

Like many of you, I love my child and am often at odds with my boss. Anybody relate? Near as I can tell, the main reason I've survived is I learned that the key self-leadership skill is figuring out how to make peace with imperfection.

Fallibility is our birthright as human beings, and learning to live within my limitations has made me a lot less stressed out, solo entrepreneur.

Fortunately, early on I got a lot of lessons from a rather unlikely source; my young daughter, Jazmine.

(Slide: A picture montage of daughter at different stages of growing up.)

Fortunately, Jazz has grown up with a resiliency and resourcefulness that's right in line with what business growth expert, Brian Tracey, expounds upon when he says,

"Difficulties are placed in our path, not to obstruct, but to instruct."

For whatever reason, we're placed in each other's path today, in a way that I hope will be both instructive and interactive. I invite you (heck, I implore you) to participate. However, if for whatever reason, an exercise doesn't feel right for you, please know it's OK to pass. With that said, don't pass up an opportunity to learn by observing and encouraging other's attempts. If questions come up, rest assured there'll be a chunk of time at the end for a lively Q&A, and if you have a burning need beforehand for clarification, or a brilliant comment, fire away using the chat box. One word of warning: Please don't make your questions too complex. I crumble under pressure!

OK, here's the bad news. It's a juggle out there, and it's tough to get a grip on overload and overwhelm when there are always more items on our didn't-do list than there are hours in the day.

(Slide: Me juggling five balls.)

The good news is, I think I've come up with a framework that can let me lay out in clear, concrete terms how a group of consenting adults can practice safe stress! My goal is to give you some practical ways to refresh and refocus via a series of simple exercises that, if nothing else, will ensure that you get some serious R&R (release and recharge).

Stress rarely reaches an unsafe level when people keep problems in perspective by using their sixth sense (the sense of humor). So, here's the game plan: we're going to laugh and learn our way through six, time-tested R&R tools and techniques to decrease job tension, increase career con-

fidence, enhance personal effectiveness, and propel professional productivity.

*(Slide: "Other than that I don't have much to
offer you.")*

Heck, if you really stay light and humor me on all the
interactive exercises, I'll even throw in a lucky number seven
bonus tip, no extra charge!

OK, here's your chance to fully participate and really
get your money's worth out of this webinar. So, are you
ready? Take a deep breath. That's it folks, that's all I'm asking of you is one deep breath. A quiet, peaceful breath of
pure, natural air.

*(Slide: A tranquil lake exuding the natural beauty
of water and mountains.)*

It's a luxury we rarely allow ourselves, especially
when we're feeling stressed, which perversely is just when
we need it most. So, go ahead, take another slow, deep, oxygen rich breath. Indulge yourself. Feels good doesn't it?

OK, one last one, on me, and this time really fill your
lungs and feel them expand in your chest. As you let the air
out, let your stomach slowly sink down and really, deeply
relax.

Tip One. Stress reduction is only one deep breath
away. What a relief!

I don't know about you, but a lot of us carry a knot of
anxiety in our gut that results in rapid, shallow breathing.
Somehow we buy into the society-wide belief that the best
way to deal with being stressed out is to speed up. Which is,

of course, completely contradictory, but hey, welcome to the human race where winning is all about sprinting faster than everyone around you.

(Slide: A race with runners straining to be the first to cross the finish line.)

I don't think it's just a coincidence that *unrest* is such a close rhyme with *stressed*. Sure, sometimes you have to sprint to meet a deadline, but rushing around on a regular basis and telling yourself, and anyone who'll listen, that you're so harried, you haven't got time to breathe is no way to live a balanced life (let alone exercise the self-control and good self-leadership a successful part-time professional has to practice).

Heck, what's the point of lifting yourself out of the rat race if you never let yourself slow down enough to enjoy the view? Sure, some mornings you've got to get up and smell the coffee, but there's always a moment in the afternoon when you can literally, or figuratively, stop and smell the roses. I mean, isn't that the real beauty of working part-time? You get to make a living and still have a life!

(Slide: Photo of blooming pink rose bushes.)

Now, I know most of this is just common sense, but I also know it is not common practice. As simple as it is to ease tension by taking a few deep breaths, how many of us can honestly say we tap into this most basic form of stress management on a daily basis? We know it's good for us. But it's not sexy or high-tech, so most of us tend to give it short shrift. And some of us get seduced by quick fixes with fancy names and fabulous claims like "double debit" (decrease your debt by increasing your purchases); and "diet-tonics" (how to eat more, and weigh less).

Let's face it folks, stress can make us stupid! And if we're trying to make it part-time in this economy, we forget, at our peril, that stress is a serious adversary that can cost us dearly. But basic stress prevention doesn't have to cost you a lot of time, effort, and money. The key is, don't underestimate the foe and don't overlook freely available resources.

Each of the six R&R tips I promised you can all be done in sixty seconds or less. And last time I looked, taking a slow, relaxing, deep breath doesn't cost a dime. Part-time, *schmart*-time! In a down economy, it's a full-time job not to get down on ourselves for not doing more faster and better. And as I'll bet a lot of you have learned, it's a slippery slope from being self-critical to feeling so stressed out, you can't go to sleep.

(Slide: Sheep trying to fall asleep by counting shepherds.)

So, here's one final, and maybe most critical, benefit of breathing more slowly and deeply. It predisposes you to be more receptive to rest and relaxation, which sure makes it a whole lot easier to go to bed at night and get a sound eight hours of sleep. Waking up refreshed and revitalized is a great way to start the day. All your resources are replenished and your mind is clear and sharp. By contrast, if you're anything like yours *unruly*, when you don't get a good night's sleep, you go through the whole next day groggy; feeling and sounding sleepy in a way that sure doesn't encourage confidence in potential customers or business partners

(Slide: "Snooze you lose, rested you rock!")

OK, here's a stretch, stand up. I mean it. Provided you're able, I want you to get out of your chair and be on your feet. OK, drop your shoulders and as you lower them let some stress slide off you. Now lift both shoulders as high as you can and slowly rotate them back down. Don't stretch past the point of pain. Smile, don't strain.

Once more, this time rotate them in reverse. Feels good doesn't it? I don't know why I carry so much tension in my upper back, but if I don't stop to lower them every few hours, my shoulders seem to want to creep all the way up to my ears, and surprise, surprise, they get really sore, and I get a whopping stiff neck.

That's when I supply my own low-cost, do-it-yourself scalp massage. Here's how it works. You fold your hands behind your head, lazily interlacing your fingers like you're lying in a hammock at a ritzy Hawaiian hotel. Hey, to paraphrase Yogi Berra, 50 percent of stretching is physical the other 60 percent is having a wicked good imagination!

Alright, kidding aside, take your thumbs and place them pointing down against the base of your scalp. Now press them firmly against your body and begin to trace a slowly expanding circle. Lower your head, and keep rubbing in a circular motion into the top of your neck where so much tension gets stored. For extra credit, as you knead the tightest spots, smile. OK, finish with a deep breath in and let it out with a sigh.

*(Slide: "Ahhh! Self-massage... your body thanks
you and your psyche says you're worth it!")*

Self-care is a vital part of self-leadership. And as
promised, all together those three small acts of self-love
(breathing, shoulder roll, and self-massage) took less than a
minute to accomplish. We may not be little kids anymore,
but we still suffer if we sit too long without giving ourselves
a stretch break. It's vital to our growth personally and professionally that we don't operate just from the neck up. In
this economy, to succeed part-time we need to use both our
heads and our guts. If you only rely on the former, you're
cutting off half your assets. Literally, and figuratively, it's
important to be flexible and to be able to think fast on your
feet.

(Slide: "To err is human. To recover, divine!")

Plus, from a purely practical standpoint, case studies
have consistently proven that people come across better on
the phone when they're standing up than they do when they
are sedentary, especially when their muscles are all cramped
from being cooped up all day behind a desk.

I hope I'm preaching to the choir. If you haven't already, you may now be seated. Don't get me wrong, I get
that it's a lot more comfortable to learn sitting down, so I'm
happy for you to stay in your chair from here on out. My
point is that it's important to remember to periodically shift
things around so you avoid getting tense and don't come off
all uptight. Sometimes all it takes to refresh and refocus my
attention can be as simple as going to get a drink of cold wa-

ter or a cup of hot tea. Hey, when it comes to hydrating, I'm an equal opportunity enjoyer!

(Slide: An alluring array of healthy beverages.)

I've found out firsthand that a stretch, as deceptively simple as just getting up and making sure I drink several glasses of water during my workday, has a decidedly positive impact on my mental acuity and physical health.

Weather permitting, just going for a short walk is a wonderful way to get the best of both stress-reduction techniques, simultaneously stretching your legs and filling your lungs with fresh air. And this time of year, there's the added bonus of seeing colorful fall foliage. Heck, don't just see it, savor it. Take in the beauty of nature like a big, slow, deep breath of grateful contentment.

(Slide: Photo of lush red maple trees.)

Tip Two. In sum, it's better to stretch than to *kvetch*. Loosening our muscles is good for what ails us. It keeps our bodies supple and our brains flexible. In short, if we want our neurons to fire, we've got to oil our joints! With any luck, making a habit of doing so will keep life enjoyable well into our eighties and nineties.

As I've gotten older, one thing that definitely keeps my mind limber is to keep learning new tools from different traditions. This **Tip Three** comes care of a short meditation practice I do just about daily that I first heard about from a Vietnamese peace activist named Thich Nhat Hanh, who once told a roomful of restless CEO's at a Buddhist retreat center in California, "Don't just do something, sit there!"

The good news is that for **Tip Three** you can stay sitting comfortably in your chair, and you can even close your eyes. It's a guided imagery exercise I adapted from one of Thich Nhat Hanh's best-loved meditations.

(Slide: "Sometimes we're smiling because we are
serene, and sometimes we become serene by
smiling." ~ Thich Nhat Hanh)

Basically, it combines four sentences with four peaceful smiles. I know that many smiles is a tough job but hey, somebody's got to do it! The first one goes like this. "Breathing in, I calm my body. Breathing out, I smile." I'll repeat the words; your part is to time your breathing accordingly. Remember, you're welcome to close your eyes. And if you want to follow along with the text, that's fine too. Each sentence I speak will show up as a new slide on your screen. Alright, make yourself comfortable, and let out a long, slow exhalation. Here we flow...

Breathing in, I calm my body
Breathing out I smile
Breathing in I calm my body and empty my brain
Breathing out I smile and ease my burden
Breathing in I calm my body, empty my brain, and relax all tension
Breathing out I smile, ease my burden, and release all toxins
Breathing in I calm, empty, and relax my body
Breathing out I smile, ease, and release

OK, time for a quick poll on how this guided meditation changed your stress level.

Please vote (only once) from the following four choices:

A.) No noticeable difference

B.) Slight but promising shift for the better

C.) Strong, positive improvement

D.) Entered nirvana and now floating on a cloud of cosmic bliss

OK, true confession: I'm sharing all this information with you about relieving tensions and finding ways to get calmer and centered because I've learned the hard way that working for myself can be a treat, but it can also be a trap. The hidden danger of stress is that it saps self-esteem, and if unchecked, can spawn a vicious spiral of diminished confidence and coping skills (that in my case led to a major depression).

I didn't even see it coming. Before I knew it, I got sucked into trying to measure up to others' expectations and definitions of success. But it taught me that the way society's set up, it's a big challenge to be part-time and still have full self-respect. Through prolonged dry spells that sorely tested my resolve, I learned the hard way that self-leadership is having the courage to trust individual convictions and set my own standards.

Stretching and smiling, taking time to breathe deeply, these aren't complex or expensive tools. They're simple, readily accessible techniques, yet one of the most confounding parts of being human is that when it comes to putting theory into practice, simple isn't easy. Great principles don't take root without great persistence. Nothing truly worthwhile happens overnight. It takes time, tolerance, and tenacity; practice makes progress. Best of all, if you stick with it, you not only get it, you get a good feeling about yourself for not being a quitter.

(Slide: Spelling out "when we endure, we mature.")

There will now be a large collective sigh of relief, because for the next few minutes I'm not going to ask you to stretch, literally or figuratively. Instead, I'm going to invite you to settle back into one of the most time-honored learning traditions, and let me tell you a fable with a timely moral. It's called *The Parable of the Two Pots.*

A water bearer in India had two large pots. Each hung on the ends of a pole, which he carried across his neck. One of the pots had a crack in it. The other was perfect and always delivered a full portion of water. At the end of the long walk from the stream to the house, the cracked pot arrived only half full. For a good two years this pattern continued daily. Of course the perfect pot was proud of its accomplishments, how well its performance fulfilled its purpose. But the cracked pot felt ashamed that it was only realizing half of what it was made to deliver. One day its failure weighed so heavily, it spoke to the water bearer beside the stream.

(Slide: A peaceful, flowing stream.)

"I know I disappoint you every day, spilling half of the load you fill me with. I want to apologize for this crack in my side that causes the water to slowly leak out all the way back to your house. You work hard carrying me and my brother back and forth several times a day. But because of my flaw, you don't get back the full value of your efforts."

The water bearer smiled gently and said in a soft voice, "It is your crack that allows the light to come into you. Did you ever wonder about the many different kinds of flowers along your side of the path? It is no coincidence that none grow on the other pot's side. I always knew about your flaw and because of it I only planted seeds on your side of the path. Every day you faithfully water them and the colorful flowers, they bloom. For two years my house has been blessed with beautiful flower arrangements because of your dedicated service. Without you being just the way you are, my tables would not be graced with such beauty."

(Slide: An ornate vase with colorful floral arrangement.)

Each of us has our own unique flaws. We're all cracked. But it's the crack that lets our light come forth. And it's the diversity of our flaws that make our lives together so interesting, challenging, and rewarding. The trick is to take each person as they are, understand what they are capable of doing, and look for the good in their potential. More often than not, the problems we think are "the pits" prove to be portals. And when we learn to look at our own, and others', flaws in a kinder light, it frees us to have the flexibility to see that pits are also seeds.

Blessed are the flexible, for they shall not be bent out of shape!

The morale of this story is easy to remember. **Tip Four** can be summed up in just three short words: Don't complain, reframe!

(Slide: "Pits are also seeds!")

The protagonist, the water bearer, could have easily looked at the crack as a curse; instead he turned it into a blessing. The part-time path you're choosing isn't always going to be smooth. It's gonna have its ruts and cracks. When stuff leaks, the lens you look at it with is your choice. You can feel put upon and persecuted, or you can stay positive and be proactive. The former is a prescription for pessimism and resignation. The latter is a recipe for resiliency and resourcefulness.

(Slide: "Whiners complain, winners reframe, and turn adversity into opportunity.")

What I love about the water bearer is he responded to the crack not with denial, resistance, or resentment but with compassion. When we deny, we deaden. When we resist acceptance, we risk resentment. And by complaining, all we're doing is chaining ourselves to the impediment; fixating on the problem, instead of focusing on finding a solution.

Bottom line: we all get hit with business setbacks, which we can decry and dispute or accept and adapt. The water bearer chose the latter, reframed the cracked pot as friend, not foe, and found a way to leverage the leak to his benefit. WHOOPS!

(Slide: "When humans overcome obstacles, Providence smiles!")

Acronyms and aphorisms aside, the core of stress management is picking your battles wisely. Nobody can win 'em all, and a big secret to having less stress and more zest is to let go of stuff you can't be responsible for, and give it all you've got in the areas you can positively impact. So, **Tip Four** is to come up with your own twist on the Serenity Prayer. The most common version of which goes...

> *(Slide: "God grant me the serenity to accept the things I can't change, the courage to change the things I can... and the wisdom to know the difference.")*

The variation that works for me jumps straight to the request for wisdom and prays for a mature balance of perspective and priorities. The words I say to myself (sometimes several times a day) are...

> *[Slide: "God grant me the wisdom to not get all wound up about things I can't control anyway, the courage to shift what's within my sphere of influence for the better, and the maturity to pick my battles. (Amen!)"]*

Experiment and utilize whatever variant works for you to stay centered. Finding the right words is rarely easy. So, don't worry if the phrases take a while to sort out and settle in. Rest assured the word choices aren't nearly as essential as making the choice to evolve and persistently apply a variation that recalls your highest priorities and reinforces your better angels. Anything that helps you become more conscious, and more conscientious, about putting your principles and priorities into practice will be a boon.

(Slide: "What you focus on, you feed.")

Adapting the Serenity Prayer has helped me feel more centered and more congruent. Tuning into our inner compass is a core practice of Kind Management, which leads to more Kindful Communication. It's been a highly pragmatic way to build my capacity to communicate using the three C's of Kindful Communication: clarity, compassion, and composure.

Again, I invite you to explore whatever self-talk works best in your world. But remember, the only way this fourth tip is going to make your world have less stress and more zest is to print and post it where it'll serve as a regular reminder.

(Slide: "When you write it, you invite it.")

For extra reinforcement, recite it aloud a couple times a day, and it'll become an internalized affirmation that's like an emotional GPS you can always tune into for guidance. The goal is to have it become so second nature that when you're hit by a big stress storm, it's both a compass and a rudder.

(Slide: "What we appreciate, we cultivate.")

Thankfully, when it comes to putting problems in perspective and staying proactive, **Tip Five** is quick and painless — laugh! I mean it. Pretend this is a hilarious moment and make your belly rock with raucous laughter. Yeah I know, for a lot of you that felt forced and phony. But guess what? Your lungs loved it anyway. And no matter how much our brains know it's faked, our bodies can't tell the difference.

It's true. Scientists have found the body's physical response to laughter, real or contrived, is nearly identical. Now stay with me on this because it only gets better. Hey, who needs a punch line; you can cut right to the comic crux and crack up laughing for no reason (and give your organs a great aerobic workout to boot!). The practice actually has an official name, laughter yoga, and a worldwide organization, Laughter Yoga International. (Who could make this up?)

While at first blush it may sound weird, bordering on warped, it turns out viewing laughter as a form of yoga makes both spiritual and medical sense. I mean, you don't have to have government-funded research to know a good laugh eases anxiety, clears our head, and gives our spirit some breathing space. And more often than not, when our heart stays light, our head thinks more flexibly.

(Slide: "The reason angels can fly is because they take themselves lightly." ~ G.K. Chesterton.)

As my grandmother used to say to me in her thick Yiddish accent, "Robbie, you don't need to be a rabbi to know that what soap is to the body, laughter is for the soul." Which makes me think there should be some new reality TV show called "When Life Stinks… Humor is the Best Deodorant." Of course, to tune in you'd have to have HBO!

Now you may, or may not, have thought that pun was funny. It doesn't matter. Because the real beauty of laughter yoga is that it completely bypasses any need for a great line, clever joke, comic prank, or hilarious story. And according to noted humorologist, Loretta Laroche, laughter may be the best way to "prevent hardening of the attitude and stop global whining!" (Both of which she takes great comic aim at in her terrific PBS special, *Life Is Not a Stress Rehearsal*.)

Here's how it works. I'll walk you through a fun beginner practice guaranteed to release all kinds of healthy hormones and endorphins that'll boost your immune system, lower your blood pressure, relieve skeletal tension, and restore virginity!

(Slide: "Laughter is the best medicine...
plus, no co-pays!")

Step one, is to smile. Some of you are already ahead of me. Step two, is to slightly extend your smile and start to feel a small wave of laughter rolling up in your belly. Now, widen your smile into a grin that's pregnant with humor. Feel the baby laugh bouncing around in your belly. Ladies, grin even broader because you know this impish infant that's about to be born will actually be a painless childbirth!

(Slide: "Laughter, life's best antacid and
muscle relaxant!")

OK, here comes the delivery. Your smile widens expectantly as it feels this bubbling bundle of joy rising up your chest, filling your throat, and bursting out of your mouth with the sound that gives it life. A big, happy laugh reverberating with unabashed childlike glee!

I hope you humored me and feel like a proud parent. I hope even more that you enjoyed laughing just for the pure health of it. I hope as well (what can I tell ya, I'm just a hopeful guy; what a concept for a motivational humorist!), that this small taste of laughter yoga piques your appetite to learn more about the healing power of humor, and how you can use more jest to be less stressed. Here's a quick excerpt from an article I wrote called *Boosting Our Immune System by Strengthening Our Sixth Sense — the Sense of Humor:*

"Humor helps us hang tough in hard times. Laughter is nature's leavening agent. Finding the funny side gives us a lift because it relieves some of the weight of frustration. Having a sense of humor is like going through life with a built-in shock absorber. Short of severe medical or emotional tragedy, if we can laugh at it... we can live with it"

(Slide: "Laughter is like leavening, it helps heavy spirits rise!")

Here's some more good news for you. When we look at a problem through the lens of laughter, we see the word *stressed* is just *desserts* spelled backwards! (And if you stay light, they're fat free!) The icing on the cake is that if you take sixty seconds to laugh twice a day, just for the health of it, by the end of the week you'll feel like you shed fourteen pounds of stress.

Another way you can use this tip is to find a laughter buddy, someone you know who likes or needs to laugh, and arrange to spend all of one minute at lunch, after work, or even over the phone, where all you do is say, "One:... two... three..." crack up, and laugh away together till the timer goes off (or your boss gives you the hairy eyeball).

(Slide: "Fake it till you make it. More jest equals less stressed!")

I know this works because I have a friend who does it with me regularly. His first name is the same as mine, but that's where the similarity stops. Unlike your motor-mouth host, my pal, Rob Rivest, delivers his entire presentation without saying a word. Of course, what should I expect from a silent comedian? I mean, the man didn't study pantomime with Marcel Marceau in Paris for nothing (cost him hundreds of euros!). Thankfully the lessons paid off, and Rob is now a highly skilled performing artist whose talents have taken him all over the world. And luckily for me, the second I see his name on my caller ID, I'm already laughing at the irony that I'm getting a phone call from a mime!

(Slide: "Shared laughter is love made audible."
~ Izzy Gesell.)

Bottom line: it's good to laugh, and it's vital to connect. Being a part-time professional has many advantages. Being able to work on our own is very freeing, but it can also get mighty lonely. And the hard truth is that feeling separated and cut off from daily interaction with a consistent set of colleagues is a blueprint for stress.

(Slide: "Isolation is the root of distress.")

I told you earlier I suffered a bad bout of depression. What I didn't tell you is, I set myself up for it by thinking I was such a high-flyer. In my hubris, I felt I was so self-sufficient that I could do it all on my own. I couldn't, and it cost me everything I hold dear: vitality, humor, creativity, and above all, being fully present in my most cherished relationships. I had to hit bottom before I finally realized I needed to reach out, reconnect, and remember how to laugh.

(Slide: "Laughter is the shortest distance between two people.")

Please don't make the same mistake. Beware the insidious effects of isolation, and don't underestimate the foe of working alone.

Tip Six. Recognize how important it is to stay connected with kindred spirits and make sure you create mutual support systems. Take these words to heart, and rest assured that whatever you do part-time won't lead to a full-time depression like mine.

Heck, I care about this so much I practically want you to promise me that as you pursue the path of being a part-time professional, you'll make sure to maximize the excellent support The Association for Part-time Professionals has to offer you. Tell you what, just for considering keeping that promise, I'm going to make good on mine to throw in a lucky number seven bonus point; **Tip Seven** is based on the fifth habit of Stephen Covey's groundbreaking bestseller, *The Seven Habits of Highly Effective People.*

(Slide: Habit Seven — Seek first to understand before trying to be understood.)

I've witnessed professionally, and personally, that empathy is the elixir of excellent relationships. Listening carefully, and ensuring full understanding of what you heard is a vital first step. No reply gets off on a good foot without an accurate read on what the speaker is sharing. Indeed, the quickest way to sabotage an empathetic connection is rushing to respond with what you want the other person to understand, without first reflecting what you thought they wanted to communicate.

(Slide: "Validate before you advocate.")

Caring, listening, and careful summarizing are the key prerequisites for moving from the Golden Rule to what author Tony D'Alessandro coined "The Platinum Rule." Here's the distinction. The traditional Golden Rule is all about doing for others, as you would have them do unto you. The Platinum Rule puts it differently: "Do unto others the way they would prefer it was done." The former has proven a timeless credo for fairness. The latter is a cutting-edge recipe for high-trust relationships.

Case in point, last January I wanted to do something special for my partner Jeannette's birthday. My first idea for a present was to apply the Golden Rule and gift unto her, as I'd like her to gift unto me (box seats at a Celtics game in the Boston Garden). Wrong! Apparently, for all its deserved reputation for fairness, when it comes to presents the Golden Rule is a recipe for projection and rampant narcissism.

Thankfully, the Platinum Rule provided my salvation. By focusing on Jeannette's desires first, I quickly realized that a trip to a prized natural park would be far more fitting (and more happily received than tickets to a basketball game by a country mile!).

(Slide: Photo of me lifting Jeanette in my arms at base of waterfalls.)

So in the end, it's all about going back to nature! (And knowing how to nurture your relationships with others by "taking the fifth" of Covey's seven habits.) Bottom line: By seeking first to understand and deepening your level of empathy by applying the Platinum Rule, your professional and personal lives will both reap big dividends.

In closing, here's a quick recap of the seven steps in order.

Tip One: *Simplify.* Slow and steady wins the race. (Remember: Stress reduction is just one deep breath away.)

Tip Two: *Stretch.* Supple body, sharp mind. (Remember: A sure way to keep your neurons firing is keep your joints oiled.)

Tip Three: *Smile.* Stay sunny, stay calm, and stay centered. (Remember: Sometimes we're smiling because we're happy, and sometimes we're happy because we're smiling.")

Tip Four: *Shift.* Don't complain, reframe. Pits are also seeds. (Remember: The story of the water bearer in India and how he turned the cracked pot's defect into a crack delivery mechanism to line his path with blooming flowers.)

Tip Five: *Sixth Sense.* Laughter. More jest equals less stressed. (Remember: Laughter is like leavening, it helps heavy spirits rise.)

Tip Six: *Support.* Build a network of trusted allies, and you can go it on your own without having to feel alone. (Remember: Isolation is the root of distress and success cherishes camaraderie!)

Tip Seven: *Seek.* First to understand before trying to get understood. (Remember: People who apply the Platinum

Rule drink deeply from the relationship rich elixir of empathy.)

Here's a toast to your solo success, and our shared good fortune. *L'chaim*! To life, liberty, and the pursuit of part-time professionals for *big*-time results!

About Rob Peck

Rob Peck is the founder of Zestworks, a speaking and training company whose guiding belief is that high spirits mean low attrition, and when workplace morale goes up, energized job performance fuels organizational growth. (It's a shocking concept!)

Taking a balanced approach to higher education, Mr. Peck attended both the University of Pennsylvania, and the Antic Arts Academy; graduating the former Phi Beta Kappa, and the latter Magna Cum Looney! A recipient of the International Jugglers Association's Excellence in Education award, Rob's moving presentations defy convention and gravity.

He has been honored with numerous public speaking awards, and is a three-time winner of Toastmaster International's Humorous Speech Contest. Other highlights of his forty-year career include a long running one man show, commissioned by and performed at the Smithsonian Institute, as well as feature slots on cable and network television programs such as Donahue, Evening Magazine, CNBC, and Amazing America.

Rob lives in Amherst, Massachusetts, where he is an associate member of Pioneer Valley Co-Housing and coordinates their monthly First Friday Coho Concerts series. He also volunteers weekly at the pay-what-you-can Stone Soup Café and assistant coaches a youth basketball team for the South Hadley Safe Neighborhoods Initiative. Rob is regularly involved in Men's work, and deeply committed to The Mankind Project—for whom he served two years as an elected officer.

When he's not working or volunteering, Rob enjoys being outdoors, swimming or hiking, listening to live music (and being a guest performer on blues harmonica or Irish tin whistle), playing improvisational theatre games, doing Contact-Improv dancing, and is an avid golfer—whose biggest goal is to bogey every hole!

Zestwork's Speaking, Training, & Emcee Services

Rob Peck is a triple treat: riveting speaker, empowering trainer, and a multitalented emcee. Check out his program descriptions, read testimonials, and view a series of live (often humorous) two- to three-minute video highlights at www.zestworks.com.

Rob's innovative approach and fluid blend of content and comedy, combines enduring truths with mesmerizing circus skills. Bring him to keynote your event, deliver dynamic training, and add enlightening entertainment to your recognition dinner or fundraiser auction.

Zestwork's motivational programs like "Keeping All The Balls In The Air" (Tips to Get a Grip on Overload and Overwhelm) are individually designed to help leaders and teams reduce burnout, raise morale, reinvigorate commitment, and reinforce the power of collaboration.

Rob's highly adaptable employee engagement programs like "Laughter is the Best Medicine... Plus No Co-pays!" are a great way to combine a sense of purpose with a spirit of fun. Fast-paced and interactive, it empowers executives and staff to experience firsthand how humor can help companies retain, rather than constantly retrain, key personnel.

Whether you're looking to kick off a conference with something fun, fresh, and energizing, or find a motivational and uplifting training, Rob knows how to break the ice and build rapport. Thanks to his innovative preprogram Comedy Quiz he quickly identifies an audience's main stressors and pet peeves. These are then woven into an opening juggling routine that humorously depicts the daily balancing acts attendees face AND shows a clear understanding of their most pressing concerns. Throughout, Rob's gift for topical humor makes content come alive by linking lessons with laughter.

As a speaker, trainer, or emcee, Rob's literal and figurative understanding of "juggling" has helped thousands of multitasking professionals rediscover a life-balance, which frees them to have less stress and more zest at work.... and at home. From Harvard to Head Start to Hewlett Packard, Zestwork's creatively customized programs have sparked the fresh thinking and fertile collaborations that help leaders and teams stay focused, stay flexible, and stay together in a high-trust, winning organization.

Contact Information
E-mail: robpeck@zestworks.com
Phone: 413-834-3459
Web: http://www.zestworks.com

64264802R00097

Made in the USA
Charleston, SC
29 November 2016